It's been said that all houses are probably haunted—haunted with the hope and fear, the hate, lust and gallantry which their walls have enclosed. . . .

When the Morton family moved into the old Bognor House it wasn't long before several of them saw the silent figure of a woman, garbed in black, gliding around the premises.

On at least two occasions the family dog suddenly pricked up his ears, looked toward the top of the stairs, and, tail wagging, bounded up the steps. But suddenly he would cringe, and, tail between his legs, would slink back down the stairs.

Was the ghost an evil entity? Not necessarily.

Perhaps she was just a quiet Englishwoman unaware that she was dead.

A NOTE ABOUT THE AUTHOR

R. DeWITT MILLER was considered one of the world's foremost authorities on the supernormal. Through fifteen years of research he had accumulated vast files of authenticated case histories of inexplicable happenings.

His own interest in the extraordinary subject matter of this book was based on his belief that the intelligent study of mysterious and eerie happenings in every branch of science, every realm of human investigation and experience, is vital to man's understanding of his world.

IMPOSSIBLE
Yet it Happened!

Original Title: Forgotten Mysteries

by

R. DeWITT MILLER

ace books
A Division of Charter Communications Inc.
1120 Avenue of the Americas
New York, N.Y. 10036

IMPOSSIBLE—YET IT HAPPENED

Copyright, 1947 by R. DeWitt Miller

Author's dedication:

TO ELLORA, MY WIFE

The Part of This Material First Published in Coronet Magazine Is Used Here with the Permission of Esquire, Inc.

An *ACE BOOK* reprinted by arrangement
with The Citadel Press

PRINTED IN U.S.A.

Contents

Introduction

THIS BOOK is a collection of factual stories which seem impossible. It is said of Tamerlane, master of Asia and conqueror of half the world, that he only once used the word "impossible"—and that was when he was dying. Probably the fact that Tamerlane was dying is necessary to the story. A living Tamerlane would have denied using such a stupid word—and for emphasis have beheaded whoever declared otherwise.

"Impossible" is a troublesome word anyway. Perhaps it might be a good idea to limit its use—like morphine. Men can become addicted to either.

In the following pages you will encounter a number of strange incidents. You will often be sorely tempted to make use of the blessed anesthesia of "impossible." For the following stories cannot be dismissed as legend or hearsay.

They are not old wives' tales, the fantasies of barkeeps, or the meandering utterances of professional visionaries. The facts presented come from the same sources that you use every day. They are from affidavits, public records, scientific reports and publications, encyclopedias, reliable works and periodicals, statements of eminent men, etc. I have supplemented such formal research with personal investigation through interviews and correspondence. Names, places, dates are cited. In the few cases where there is a thin shadow of doubt concerning the facts, the existence of that shadow has been noted.

My basis for selecting the cases was simply the factual integrity of each story. Would a sane man, not afflicted with a desire to believe irrespective of truth, consider a given case factually strong enough to be worth mulling over?

The world is excellently supplied with professional expounders of mysteries. Many of them are honest and sincere. God knows there are enough dark corners of human experience that could stand a little expounding. Unfortunately,

7

however, the mysterious often becomes the basis for selling a bill of goods. A really good salesman needs a certain contempt for facts.

But to explain all that is mysterious by ascribing it to the doings of liars, fools, madmen and cultists is absurd.

There have been many strange occurrences in this perverse universe. You cannot pack the marvels of creation into theories with the same nicety that you pack sardines into cans. Creation is greater than what has been created, as the whole is greater than the parts.

This book is an attempt to strike a balance between openmouthed, unreasoning astonishment at miracles, and dogmatic limiting of the possible within currently accepted theories. I freely admit that the task is immemorially difficult, and that I can make no more claim to infallibility than the dogmatic "purveyors of certainties" with whom I have so often scuffled.

Another purpose of this book is to draw together the mysterious from many fields. With all our proud statements about modern enlightenment, few lines of investigation do not have their quota of startling and unexplained cases.

Because most of the following stories are stubbornly at odds with "normal" conceptions, they slipped easily from the memory of men. Sometimes they have remained in a sort of limbo. Usually they have been simply forgotten. Hence the title of this volume. It is the same as that of a monthly feature which I wrote over a period of several years for Coronet magazine. The Coronet series began in January, 1940. I wish to express my appreciation to Coronet for permission to republish certain of this material.

The majority of the stories presented in this book were among the hundreds in the Coronet series. However, a very considerable number of new cases has been added. In addition, most of the stories published in Coronet have been treated at greater length.

In Coronet no attempt was made to organize the stories. Month after month they appeared simply as unexplained and forgotten tales. Now I have made some effort at order. However, it was occasionally necessary to be arbitrary in assigning stories to the various chapters. Although the stories tend to cluster around certain nuclei, there are inevitably borderline cases which could be classified under two or more headings.

Certain of the chapters require a brief word of explanation:

"Riffraff and Rabble" is a collection of rugged individuals who refused to fit into any category. After failing to coerce them into any semblance of integration, I decided to give them a separate chapter where they could frolic undisturbed by a theme. It is conceivable that they have only taken French leave from some organized conception, but at present they are utterly intractable.

"Forgotten Experiments," although greatly enlarged, stems from a feature under that title which I conducted for some months in Coronet. As more fully discussed in the introduction to the chapter, they are experiments which, although appearing of utmost significance, received an instant of publicity and then vanished.

"Valley of the Shadow" is not intended to proselyte for any faith, creed, religion or belief. It cites some data concerning "this thing men call dying." These data concern both what happens at the moment of death and the ancient problem of immortality. It is not my intention to encourage or confound the faithful.

Each chapter has a brief introduction which supplies a background to the core of speculation around which the cases are assembled. These introductions are intended only as commentaries. Most of the fields covered by the chapters have already spawned many lusty tomes. In a book such as this exhaustive treatment is out of place. However, a certain amount of background material is necessary to fully appreciate the significance of the cases.

It was twenty odd years ago when I began the investigation of the mysterious. Since then I have encountered a number of men and women who were exploring the same enigmatic land. However, most collections of unorthodox stories are either limited to a specific type of material or else are marshaled for the purpose of supporting an explanation. The explanations of what God hath wrought and how the "wroughting" was done are manifold indeed.

In the field of general investigation of the mysterious two writers are outstanding. Lieutenant Commander Rupert T.

Gould, R.N., wrote *Oddities* and *Enigmas*. Both works are excellent.

Gould dealt with less than a dozen cases in each book, but they were taken from widely separated fields. He treated his mysteries at considerable length and with thoroughness.

Charles Fort wrote four volumes which have been assembled and republished as *The Books of Charles Fort.* His usual method was a deluge of brief, semi-related, unorthodox data. His great aim in life was to roust men out of complacent dogmatism. That in itself is a noble purpose. Evaluating Charles Fort is not a matter to be lightly undertaken.

I hereby acknowledge my debt to both the men above mentioned.

The vast majority of the cases have never appeared in any general collection of factual mysteries. Around some tumult and shouting has raged; others have appeared and disappeared quietly and obscurely.

If you ask me what I have concluded about them, I can only reply in this manner:

When William James died, and in so doing deprived America of her only truly great philospher, he left—strangely—on his desk the following statement, the last sentences he wrote:

"There is no conclusion. What has concluded that we might conclude in regard to it?"

What has?

Chapter 1

RIFFRAFF AND RABBLE

As HAS already been mentioned, "Riffraff and Rabble" has no theme whasoever. Subjects like Lost Atlantis, sea serpents, ghosts, have a vast background of speculation and theory. Not so the following stories. However, some of the cases require a brief special notation. I will take them up in the order they appear in the chapter.

Concerning the last moments in the life of Jeffery Derosier and their connection with the mirror, I have supplemented the published records by writing most of the principal witnesses, including surgical nurse Adeline Knoop. It seemed to me that she was in the best position to ascertain the truth of the matter. The replies to my inquiries—Miss Knoop's among them—substantiated the facts as I have given them. No explanation was advanced.

It is probable that recent studies of massive brain injuries —facilitated by the war—have made the cases cited by Dr. Iturricha somewhat less miraculous, although no more explainable under the accepted concepts of physiology.

The "Devil's Footprints" have given birth to several theories. Charles Fort suggested that they were not footprints at all, but rather imprints made by—as I understand him— rays shot at the earth from somewhere in space, possibly some sort of code dispatched in an effort to communicate with the earth, or with a lost expedition from another planet which met with disaster here. Several psychical researchers have blamed the occurrence on hard working poltergeists. Lieutenant Commander Rupert T. Gould suspected an unknown creature which emerged from the sea, made the footprints, and departed whence it came. I must admit that I am unimpressed by any of the theories.

Now to the stories . . .

ON THE afternoon of February 20, 1936, Jeffery Derosier lay dying in the War Memorial Hospital at Sault Ste. Marie, Michigan. His bed was in a small ward, occupied by

11

four other patients. Beside Derosier's bed was an enameled table, on which lay a plain mirror. The mirror had no back. It was just a silvered piece of glass. Derosier asked for the mirror, and the nurse handed it to him.

The occupants of the ward watched. There was no particular significance to the scene. The others in the room may have guessed that for Derosier tomorrow and tomorrow was no longer a problem.

For a moment Derosier stared into the mirror. Then he threw it on the table, crying hysterically:

"My God, I'm dying!"

There was silence. No one seemed quite able to contradict him. Finally Derosier spoke again. He said a senseless thing.

"You won't be able to pick up that mirror."

Five minutes later, and without having amplified his last words, he died.

After Derosier's body had been removed, Harvey Davenport, one of the other patients in the ward, tried to pick up the mirror. It wouldn't budge. Next the nurse tried. The mirror was immovable.

Dr. F. J. Moloney, who had been attending Derosier, tried his hand at moving the perverse piece of glass. He also failed. Nurses from other wards, interns and patients, attempted, with a variety of tools, to move the mirror. It continued to stick.

For twenty-four hours that mirror defied all efforts to move it.

The tale of the strange fulfillment of Derosier's last words spread through Sault Ste. Marie. A complete account of the mystery, including statements of witnesses, was carried by the *Evening News*. The A.P. picked it up and teletypes ground it out.

Still that ordinary mirror remained on that plain hospital table.

Dr. Moloney said he had no explanation. No one else could suggest any. All that anyone cared about was to get the damned thing off the table. Haunted mirrors do not belong in hospitals. The publicity was unwelcome.

A nurse assailed the mirror with an ice pick. She pried vigorously. The mirror would not budge. She gave up.

Next a surgical nurse named Adeline Knoop attempted to work her fingernail under the mirror. Suddenly—and seemingly of its own accord—the mirror flew several feet into the air and fell back to the floor.

It was immediately examined. There was nothing on the back which might form an adhesive. The table was dry. Replaced on the table, the mirror did not adhere. It was placed in various positions. Still it would not stick. Water was spread on the table in an effort to create a suction. But the magic was gone from the mirror. It would not stick.

Finally the mirror was "accidentally" broken. The pieces were thrown away by nurse Mrs. Grace Fleming, who said it was "good riddance." Perhaps it was.

OF ALL the tales of world-shaking inventions, none is stranger than the following:

In the early months of 1917—just before the United States entered World War I—Walter Scott Meriwether, veteran newspaperman and Navy editor for the *New York World,* was called to the office of Commander Earl P. Jessop, senior engineering officer and captain of the Brooklyn Navy Yard. Commander Jessop declared:

"I have just seen something that all my technical knowledge . . . tells me is impossible. Yet certainly my instruments of precision did not deceive me. We have just tested an invention that gives every indication of being the greatest since gunpowder."

Here is Commander Jessop's story:

Among the hopeful inventors whom it was his duty to investigate was a Portuguese named John Andrews, who lived at McKeesport, Pennsylvania. Andrews claimed that he had found a substance which, when added to either fresh or salt water, would produce a substitute for gasoline.

When Andrews drove into the Brooklyn Navy Yard, he carried a small satchel. He was given a bucket of water and an empty can which had been thoroughly inspected. With these he entered the back seat of his car. A moment later, when he returned, the bucket was empty and the can filled with what appeared to be water.

Commander Jessop personally carried the can to the Navy laboratory and dumped the contents into the gas tank of a motor boat engine. The engine had been drained of all fuel. As a final check, *over half a gallon of water* was poured into the tank along with the gallon of "fuel" Andrews had concocted. ·

The motor immediately started and ran at seventy-five per cent of maximum efficiency until Andrews' "fuel" was exhausted.

The Navy department remained highly suspicious, but asked Andrews to return the next day. *This time he was placed in a bare concrete room with no exit except a door and no drain where he could dispose of any liquid.* He was given a bucket of sea water and a gallon can. When he emerged the bucket was empty and the inspected can filled. *It was impossible for him to have disposed of the sea water except by pouring it into the can.* The contents of the can were poured into the motor *which ran as before.*

The Navy department went into a huddle and Andrews went back to McKeesport. A few days later, Secretary of the Navy Josephus Daniels sent for Andrews, but Andrews could not be found.

The rest of the story is deep in shadow. Andrews is supposed to have left hurriedly for England to negotiate with the British government. Eventually he returned to America. It is said that he became a recluse.

At the time of the original demonstration, Commander Jessop stated: *"With the precautions we had taken . . . there was no possibility of deception."*

Years later in 1935 he was still of the same opinion. It was in that year that Meriwether wrote an account of the incident—which was published in *Esquire* and *Reader's Digest.* As a double check, Meriwether sent his manuscript to Jessop, who read it and certified the complete accuracy of the facts as stated.

During the search for Andrews in 1917 his rooms were found in great disorder, and it was considered for many years that he might have been mysteriously abducted. However, it was later established that he had merely left hurriedly and secretly for England.

In 1945 I wrote Meriwether, then editor and publisher of

the *Mississippi Sun*, Charleston, Mississippi, and he replied at considerable length—once more attesting the facts. All in all, the whole matter is baffling indeed.

WHILE conducting an archeological investigation at the Temple of Old Mahableshwar in 1934, M. Paul Dare, news editor of *The Times of India*, came upon a rare image of the four-faced goddess, Gayatri. Intending to photograph this unusual find, he set up his camera and was about to take a picture when a Brahmin priest strode up and declared briefly: "You won't be able to photograph that idol."

At the time there was also present a friend of Dare's, an erudite Indian scholar and Brahmin, Mr. Vishnu Karandikar. He had also brought a camera. Using both cameras, he and Dare took several exposures of the image. When the films of both cameras were developed, the wall against which the idol stood showed sharp and clear, in good focus and excellently exposed—but there was not the faintest trace of the image.

Later the priest told them that although Dare would have little chance of photographing the idol in any case, Karandikar, being a Brahmin, could photograph it if a certain magical rite were performed. He performed the rite and then photographed the image exactly as he had done before. This time the idol appeared normally on the film.

Dare reported the whole case in detail in his *Indian Underworld*, published in 1940. He noted that Karandikar had lived long in London and was of a highly sceptical turn of mind.

CONCERNING things that can't be photographed, let's have a look at the following case.

In the Ceylon jungle two Englishmen set about the semi-prosaic job of shooting a travel film outside the time-battered temple of Katargama. The Britishers, artist Brook-Farrar and photographer G. A. Smith, were attracted by a slim, half nude dancing girl who swayed in front of what had once been a wall.

A tripod was set up, and a movie camera focused on the

figure. The girl was centered in the finder, and film began to grind past the shutter. And as the girl swayed and the film spun through the camera, natives stood by watching, half amused expressions on their faces.

Suddenly the girl vanished. So unexpected was her disappearance that the Englishmen were momentarily startled. Then, deciding that she had stepped behind a rock or tree, they packed their equipment, well satisfied.

Later they developed the film. There was the temple. There was the bright, hard sunlight. There were the amused natives. *But there was no dancing girl.* Not a frame of film carried an impression of that swaying figure which had appeared so clearly in the finder.

Far away from the dank Ceylon jungle, in the quiet, scholarly atmosphere of California's Mt. Wilson Observatory —home of the great hundred-inch reflector—famed astronomer Gustaf Strömberg examined the credentials of the story and considered it valid. He included it in his book, *Soul of the Universe,* published in 1940.

BEFORE the Anthropological Society of Sucre, Bolivia, arose prominent Bolivian physician, Dr. Augustin Iturricha. He described some startling case histories taken from the record of the clinic of his colleague, Dr. Nicholas Ortiz. Startling they were indeed.

". . . The authenticity of these observations cannot be doubted. They proceed from . . . authorities of high standing in our scientific world.

"The first case refers to a boy of twelve to fourteen years of age, *who died with full use of his intellectual faculties* though the encephalic mass was completely detached from the bulb, *a condition which amounted to real decapitation.* What must have been the stupefaction of the operators at the autopsy when, on opening the cranial cavity, they found . . . a large abscess involving nearly the whole cerebellum, part of the brain and the protuberance. Nevertheless the patient, shortly before, was known to have been actively thinking.

"Another case coming from the same clinic is that of a young agricultural laborer, eighteen years of age. The post mortem revealed three communicating abscesses, each as large as a tangerine orange, occupying the posterior of both cerebral hemispheres and part of the cerebellum. In spite of this, the patient *thought as do other men*, so much so that one day he asked for leave to settle his private affairs. He died on re-entering the hospital.

"A third case is not less unusual. It is that of a native aged forty-five years . . . The autopsy revealed a large abscess occupying nearly the whole left cerebral hemisphere. In this case also we must ask: *'How did this man manage to think?'* "

Dr. Iturricha's little question is quite apropos. A condition that amounted to decapitation—brains largely destroyed—how *did* these men manage to think?

I do not have the exact date of Dr. Iturricha's address. However, it was probably shortly before 1920. Dr. Gustave Geley, from whose work, *From the Conscious to the Unconscious*, I take the above data, indicates that the address was of recent date; Dr. Geley's work was published in 1920.

JOHN NEWTON was duly hanged in Montgomeryshire, Wales, one day in 1821. A sudden thunder storm roared during the execution. The rope jerked, the dangling body swung slowly. The case of John Newton was closed. And yet . . .

Throughout his trial Newton consistently maintained his innocence. The case against him depended upon the testimony of two prominent local citizens, both of whom had good reason to wish him a speedy return to his ancestors. When sentence of death was pronounced, he turned to the court and said quietly: "I am innocent—and no grass will grow over my grave for a generation to prove it."

No grass did. For many years the spot in the churchyard where Newton lay was marked by a sterile patch about the size and shape of a coffin. In 1852 the Rev. R. Mostyn Price published an account of the matter, saying: "Thirty years have passed away and the grass has not covered his grave."

Several attempts were made to break the curse. New seed and fresh soil were used. It did no good. The grass would not grow.

Soon after Reverend Price had written about the matter, another effort was made. This time new turf was laid down.

17

Part of this grew for a while, but that over Newton's head died at once. A few months later the rest of the grass withered—leaving the same accursed rectangle as before.

In 1886—more than a generation after Newton had climbed the gallows in a thunder storm—the bare spot, although somewhat smaller, still remained. When Christina Hole compiled her *Haunted England* in 1941, she said: "Today it [the bare spot] can be seen in the form of a distinct cross of sterile ground with the grass growing strongly round it."

And while we're on the subject of hangings, we might consider the next case, which is classic. It certainly caused enough uproar at the time.

ON THE gray, raw morning of February 23, 1895, John Lee, convicted of murdering an old woman, climbed the scaffold at Exeter, England. The noose was dropped over his head and adjusted. The sheriff signaled for the trap to be sprung.

The bolt was drawn—*but the trap did not drop.* John Lee was told to step back, and the trap was tested and found to work perfectly. Again John Lee took his place. And again the trap would not fall.

He was taken back to his cell. The trap was tested. The warden stood in the same place as John Lee, and held on to the rope. The bolt was drawn, and the trap fell as it should. John Lee was brought back from his cell and for a second time climbed the steps that no man is supposed to descend.

Twice more the bolt was drawn—and twice more the trap stood firm. The witnesses were becoming fearful of supernatural powers. The sheriff gave up. The matter was referred to the British Home Secretary. It was debated in Parliament. John Lee's sentence was commuted to life imprisonment. Some years later, and for no apparent reason, he was released.

Scores of articles have been written about "The Man They Couldn't Hang," and it has been the *casus belli* of arguments beyond number. The tale has been embellished with a number of twists. Lee is supposed to have dreamed the night before his "execution" that he could not be hanged; he is said to have been in league with a witch, etc. However, the naked facts are as given above.

A STRANGE "fog"—dark and deadly—hovered over the lowlands near Liege, Belgium, during the first days of December, 1930. For a week it was front page copy throughout the world.

On December 6, 1930, thick yellow vapor, different from any fog which residents had ever experienced, cloaked the Meuse River Valley. Those who entered the mist shrouded area were choked and suffocated. *In one day there were sixty deaths and three hundred cases of acute illness.* The hospitals of Liege became "like World War days."

People were afraid to leave their homes. They peered out into the darkness, fearing that choking death should creep their way.

The deadly miasma was at first attributed to fumes from a zinc factory, but it was soon pointed out that the zinc factory had not been in operation for months. Later there were mutterings about secret World War I gases. And then, as mysteriously as it had come, the Black Fog of death vanished. There was fog still, but it was ordinary harmless mist.

As the publicity was dying down, it was stated—as a sort of addenda—that similar death fogs had occurred in 1897, 1902, and 1911. Nothing was ever heard of any of the official investigations into the 1930 occurrence.

IT WAS 3:00 A.M. on the morning of June 10, 1909, and the Danish East Asiatic company's steamship *Bintang* was ploughing through the darkness in the Straits of Malacca, when Captain Gabe saw a vast revolving wheel of light, apparently just below the surface of the water. In his words:

"Long arms issued from a center around which the whole system appeared to rotate." So vast was the wheel that only half of it could be seen at a time, the rest lying beyond the horizon.

Captain Gabe made sure the rays of light did not come from any known source. There were no other ships in the vicinity. The rays could not be caused by the lights of the *Bintang* as the luminous arms were too vast, came from a different direction than the ship's lights, and traveled at a different speed than the *Bintang*.

The great wheel slowly approached the ship, growing dimmer and seeming to sink deeper into the water. At last it vanished.

Were there, perhaps, strange doings beneath the sea on that quiet June night? Whatever the answer, the record is in a publication of the Danish Meteorological Institute.

IF YOU enjoy explaining things, you might draw lance and joust merrily with the *Devil's Footprints*.

On the morning of February 8, 1855, the citizens of a number of towns in South Devon, England, discovered strange tracks in the snow. The tracks were found in and about the towns of Topsham, Lympstone, Exmouth, Teignmouth, and Dawlish. In all, they *covered more than a hundred miles.* They did not resemble anything the good burghers of South Devon had ever seen. The tracks were four inches in length and two and three-quarters in breadth; they were shaped rather like a hoof print.

The shape and size of the prints were, however, the least mysterious of the circumstances surrounding them. For whatever the "creature" that made them, it was able to go wherever it chose, regardless of intervening obstacles.

A report of the occurrence published in the *London Times* of February 16, 1855, states: "The mysterious animal must have been endowed with the power of ubiquity, as the footprints were seen *in all kinds of inaccessible places*—on the tops of houses and narrow walls, in gardens and courtyards enclosed by high walls and palings, as well as in open fields. There was hardly a garden in Lympstone where the hoof prints were not observed."

One eye witness stated: "The regular track (*the distance between the footprints was always exactly eight inches*) passed in some instances over the roofs of houses and hayricks, and very high walls (one fourteen feet), *without displacing the snow on either side or altering the distance between the prints.*"

Naturally the track of an unknown animal which suddenly appears in a highly populated region is a startling occurrence. But when the animal can cover a hundred miles in a single night, cross roofs without awakening anyone in the houses, pass over walls as if they did not exist, and even span a large body of water, "startling" ceases to be an appropriate word.

Nevertheless, all that was still the least of the problem, *for the tracks were in a straight line.*

No known creature, not even man, makes regular footprints in a straight line. Bipeds may hop on one foot for a short distance, but not for a hundred miles. Galloping quadrupeds sometimes leave what superficially appears to be a track in a straight line, but close examination will show the separate feet. Moreover, no quadruped could gallop *at a constant pace* for over a hundred miles.

Then we come to the matter of the regular spacing of the tracks. In one of the reports of the occurrences published in the *Illustrated London News* for February 24, 1855, it is stated that the spacing of eight inches between the prints *was invariable "in every parish."*

In places it appeared that the snow had been removed rather than pressed down. Many of the tracks looked "as if branded with a hot iron." Several drawings of the tracks were reproduced in the *Illustrated London News.* All of them show the prints in a straight line.

The publicity immediately following the occurrence ended on a queer note. On March 17, 1855, the *Illustrated London News* carried an item from a correspondent in Heidelberg. He stated "upon the authority of a Polish Doctor of Medicine" that on a sand hill in Russian Poland but near the border of Galicia such strange tracks were often seen, both in the snow and the sand of the hill. He said the tracks "are attributed by the inhabitants to supernatural influences."

Whatever the cause of the marks in the snow of South Devon, the inhabitants double bolted their doors for many weeks. But the "tracks" never reappeared. The people of South Devon gave up explaining. They simply referred to the marks as "The Devil's Footprints." Perhaps that "explanation" is as good as any.

WILLIAM JAMES, sometime American philosopher and psychologist, investigated many strange tales, such as the case of Lurancy Vennum.

Lurancy Vennum, who lived with her parents in Watseka,

Illionois, was a normal girl until one day in 1887, during her fourteenth year, when she suddenly fell into a profound sleep. From this she awakened as a completely new personality. The new personality said it was that of Mary Roff, who had died in Watseka twelve years before.

The girl immediately took up residence with the Roff family, where she was found to have those memories which the dead girl would be expected to possess. For fifteen weeks she led the life of Mary Roff, claiming steadfastly that she had recrossed the "moment of shadow" and borrowed the body of Lurancy Vennum. And during all those weeks, her every mannerism, memory, and attitude was that of the dead girl.

After the fifteen weeks, she said that she was returning to the "other world." The girl again entered a trance-like condition. When she awakened, she was Lurancy Vennum.

If the whole thing was some strange, senseless masquerade, then Lurancy Vennum had, at fourteen, investigated Mary Roff's past with a thoroughness that would do honor to the world's best secret service. There was evidence too that she possessed information which would be known only to Mary Roff.

If it were not a masquerade . . . After all, the idea that one soul can "possess" another's body is deep in the background of the race. James was still puzzling over the case when he passed through the door which Mary Roff claimed to have reopened.

THE GREAT darkness over New England remains a perplexing phenomenon. The intensity of the gloom, its lengthy duration, the great area covered, all set the occurrence apart from other periods of abnormal darkness.

May 19, 1780, dawned clear and warm over New England. At 10:00 A.M. a haze formed in the southwest. Traveling with the wind, this overcast rapidly spread north-eastward. Within an hour it had reached the Canadian border. Following the haze, thick darkness settled over the land.

As the blackness deepened, candles were lit and torches appeared in the streets. At noon the schools were dismissed, and the people of New England became awe-stricken at the profound darkness at midday. But it was only the beginning.

By one o'clock the blackness was that of a starless midnight. Apprehension became fear, and fear panic. Churches were opened and soon crowded with the devout—and the fearful. Ministers expounded mightily on the Day of Judgment.

The darkness covered what are now the states of Maine, New Hampshire, Vermont, Massachusetts, Rhode Island, and Connecticut. Eastern New York, and northeastern Pennsylvania were also within the area of blackness.

In Hartford the Connecticut legislature was in session. By noon the members were unable to see each other, and the session threatened to break up in panic. At this point one of the members, Mr. Davenport, arose: "Mr. Speaker, this is either the Day of Judgment, or it is not. If it is not, there is no need for adjourning. If it is, I desire to be found doing my duty. I move that candles be brought in, and that we proceed to business."

By late afternoon a sheet of white paper held within a few inches of the eyes was invisible. As the scene was later described by John Greenleaf Whittier, ". . . men prayed and women wept, all ears grew sharp to hear the doom-blast of the trumpet shatter the bleak sky."

During the period when the blackness was deepest, an eerie light was reported. Objects seen in the glow of torches appeared in unnatural colors. Particularly noted was a faint greenish hue which seemingly filtered through the gloom. Later even this strange light faded, leaving only the blackness of eternal night.

A full moon was due to rise at 9:00 P.M., but the blackness overhead remained unbroken. Finally, at 1:00 A.M., May 20, the first wisp of light was seen. It was the moon, high in the sky and blood red. Shortly afterwards stars appeared. At daybreak the sun rose as clear and bright as it had twenty-four hours before. The strange darkness had lasted fourteen hours.

Those who had experienced New England's *Black Friday* were thankful indeed for friendly, normal sunlight.

Chapter 2

PHANTOM ARMIES

DURING World War I there were vast commotions about phantom armies and visions in the sky seen during the early months of the conflict. The occurrences were variously titled "The Angels of Mons," "St. George," "The Phantom Bowmen of Agincourt," "Joan of Arc," etc.

An explanation was soon brought forward by Arthur Machen, British writer, who said the basis of the whole thing was a story of his, "The Bowmen," which he claimed to have composed in a church while the deacon was singing the gospel. This explanation crashed on a small matter of dates. The story was not published until September 29, 1914, and all accounts of the visions agreed that they occurred during the last days of August.

Of these alleged visions of August, 1914. I have selected the incidents which are best documented.

The very interesting case of the White Cavalry at Bethune was first given general publication in 1940, and has been largely lost sight of. By 1940 another World War had been started and phantoms from World War I were outmoded. This case is particularly intriguing because it occurred in 1918, nearly four years after the original outburst of specters.

All in all, there is much evidence that *something*—mass hypnosis, accumulated psychic power, a break in the continuity of Time, extra-dimensional spectators at our big show, or perhaps, even, angelic visitors—was breaking the laws of normalcy during those blood-drenched days of August, 1914. The case in 1918 indicates that such strange occurrences may have been repeated.

The story of the cross seen in the sky of England during World War II has nothing to do with phantom armies, but it seems to be of the same ilk. It was given considerable publicity at the time. The only explanations I have heard were mumblings about "suggestion" and "hysteria." The case is a good example of how easily and quickly such matters pass into the limbo of the "forgotten."

By the end of August, 1914, endlessly advancing Germans had destroyed the Allies' last illusions of early victory. In those days of retreat, weariness, death, and burning sunlight, queer tales began to be told.

Nurses and officers in the field reported having heard versions of these stories, varying only in minor details, from hundreds of witnesses. Unknown thousands of other witnesses gave no testimony at all. After those August days they ceased to testify to anything—except, perhaps, the accuracy of the enemy's fire.

Of the published accounts I have selected the following three:

Lance Corporal Headly-Johns of the Lancashire Fusiliers first described the occurrence to a nurse, who repeated it to a superintendent of the Red Cross, Miss M. Courtney Wilson. A few weeks later Johns was interviewed on leave by London newspaperman Harold Begbie. Here is Johns' statement:

"I was in my battalion in the retreat from Mons on or about August 28 . . . The weather was very hot and clear, and between eight and nine o'clock in the evening I was standing with a party of nine other men on duty . . . Captain Leaton suddenly came up to us in a state of great anxiety and asked us if we had seen anything startling (he used the word 'astonishing') . . .

". . . afterwards Captain Leaton came back, and taking me and some others a few yards away, showed us the sky. I could see quite plainly in mid-air a strange light which seemed to be quite distinctly outlined and was not a reflection of the moon, nor were any clouds in the neighborhood.

"The light became brighter and I could see quite distinctly three shapes, one in the center having what looked like spread wings. The other two were not so large but quite plainly distinct from the center one. They appeared to have a long loose hanging garment of gold tint, and they were above the German lines and facing us.

"We stood watching them for about *three-quarters of an hour*. All the men with me saw them, and other men came up from other groups who also told us they'd seen the same thing. I am not a believer in such things, but I have not the slightest doubt but that we really did see what I now tell you . . . I have a record of fifteen years good service, and I should be very sorry to make a fool of myself by telling a story merely to please anyone."

On the night of August 28, 1914, a nurse, Miss Phyllis Campbell, a cousin of Lady Archibald Campbell, was attending a wounded R.F.A. man who told her: "We all saw it. First there was a yellowish mist sort of rising before the Germans as they came to the top of the hill. I just gave up. No use fighting the whole German race . . . The next minute comes this funny cloud of light, and when it clears off there's a táll man with yellow hair and golden armour on a white horse, holding his sword up. Before you could take a breath, the Germans had turned and we were after them."

"Could you see the face?" asked Miss Campbell.

"Yes, it was very clear. As plain as I see you now."

Miss Campbell heard the same story from scores of soldiers. A month later she received a letter from a woman friend in Germany, a nurse at the Potsdam Hospital. The hospital was then crowded with German wounded. The letter read:

"There has been much comment here because a certain regiment which had been ordered to take a small section of the front failed to carry out commands. It was impossible, the officers declared!

"When they went forward they were powerless; their horses turned sharply around and fled. Nothing could stop them. 'We saw at the same moment strange shapes in the sky, and lower down a huge man on a white horse . . . It was like going full speed ahead and being suddenly pulled up in front of a precipice.' That is the way they talk. Is there something to it, Phyllis?"

Then there is one quiet little statement, devoid of all sound and fury, which was made by an officer, Lieutenant Colonel F. E. Seldon, in a letter to the *London Evening News*, September 14, 1915.

Lieutenant Colonel Seldon stated that on the night of August 27, 1914, he was with two other British officers just ahead of their weary column. As they rode along, Seldon watched in amazement a long cavalcade of horsemen which paralleled the column on both sides. The night was not very dark.

Thinking the whole matter a delusion, Lieutenant Colonel Seldon refrained from mentioning it to the other officers. After about fifteen minutes, one of them asked whether Seldon saw squadrons of strange white cavalry riding parallel with them. The third officer then also admitted that he saw them. They were also seen by many men in the column.

So convinced were the officers of the reality of the cavalry that at the next halt ". . . one of us took a party of men out to reconnoiter, and found no one there."

The night then grew darker and the ghostly cavalry was no longer seen.

Lieutenant Colonel Seldon's statement closed with this paragraph: "I myself am absolutely convinced that I saw those horsemen; and I feel sure that they did not exist only in my imagination. I do not attempt to explain the mystery—I only state the facts."

The next story is, in my opinion, probably the most powerful and significant tale of ghostly armies to come from World War I.

It appeared in an English publication, *The National Message*, April 24, 1940. *The story is told first hand by a highly trained observer, Captain Cecil Wightmick Haywood, formerly staff captain, first corps British Intelligence.*

At the time of the occurrence he was stationed at the small Belgian town of Bethune. Just in front of Bethune was the famous "LaBassee front." Early in 1918, Portuguese troops were sent to this front. The Germans immediately gave them a terrific shelling. They fled, leaving a gap in the Allied lines.

To delay the German advance, squads of British machine gunners were placed along the banks of the LaBassee canal. The German artillery began shelling these machine guns, then suddenly shifted and mercilessly pounded a patch of barren ground near Bethune. Next the deserted area was raked with German machine gun fire.

"Fritz has gone balmy, sir," said a sergeant standing close to Captain Haywood. "What the hell can he be peppering that open ground for?"

Then the German firing ceased. Startled, Captain Haywood made his way to the bank of the canal. Before him masses of German infantry were fleeing in unimaginable confusion, flinging away their weapons and supplies, striving only for greater speed towards the Fatherland.

During the next few days Captain Haywood interviewed scores of prisoners, many of them officers. All told substantially the same story.

The Germans had been advancing, singing, sure of ultimate victory. Suddenly a formation of white cavalry was seen on the hill near Bethune.

In the Germans' own words: "They were all clad in white, and mounted on white horses." All the Germans saw them, including the observers for the artillery. The artillery and machine guns churned up the ground over which the strange cavalry was advancing. Concentration of fire power was frightful. *Not a white horseman fell.*

The Germans stated: "The cavalry . . . rode quietly forward at a slow trot. In front of them rode their leader—a fine figure of a man—by his side was a great sword, not a cavalry sword, but similar to those used by the Crusaders; in his hands lay quietly the reins of his white charger."

And then the pride of the Kaiser's army fled in fear—fled when the battle was won, when the Allied position was desperate, when there was nothing between the Germans and victory but a few forlorn machine guns.

As yet, no ghostly legions have been reported from the battefields of World War II. However, there is a story of the mass observation of a strange thing in the sky of England. That was in the days before the Invasion, when England's daily ration was still blood and tears.

At the end of April, 1944, London newspapers carried stories about a vision of Christ on the Cross supposedly observed in the sky by hundreds of persons at Ipswich. The vision was seen April 27 during an air raid alert. A week later the American papers picked up the story. On May 7, the *Chicago Tribune Press Service* sent out a dispatch:

". . . numerous residents of eastern England stoutly maintain that the sign of the Cross was visible in the sky for *fifteen minutes* . . . Those who have given detailed descriptions include a naval commander, a carpenter, housewives, etc. The concensus of the statements is that the vision gradually grew clearer until the figure of Christ was distinct. The local pastor is investigating . . ."

Typical accounts were published, such as that given by William Garnham, an engineer: "I saw the sign of the cross actually start to form. There was no mistake in either the shape of the crucifix or the figure nailed to it."

On May 8 the local pastor made his report, which was carried in America by both the *Associated Press* and the *United Press*. The pastor, Rev. Harold Godfrey Green, vicar of St. Nicholas Church and army chaplain, reported that during his investigation he interviewed *two thousand people*. He concluded:

"There was scarcely any variation—if any—in these accounts. I have verified the fact of the vision quite definitely. *I am satisfied myself, beyond doubt, of the authenticity of the vision.*

"There were clouds in the sky which . . . drifted by *while the vision remained stationary.*"

Chapter 3

SEA SERPENTS

COMES NOW the defendant, a sea serpent, and hereinafter makes reply to the charge of not existing.

Strictly speaking, the argument about the existence of unknown marine monsters has little to do with "sea serpents." Even the most ardent believers in such creatures do not claim that they are gigantic serpents. The real argument lies elsewhere—in the time of the dinosaur.

Geologist John Hodgdon Bradley, Jr.—University of Southern California—says in his *Parade of the Living*, "They [dinosaurs] ruled longer than any other animal before or since . . . Although eons have now rolled over their bleaching bones . . . the dinosaurs led lives of richness within the limits set upon them; they bargained well with fate."

Whether "eons have now rolled over their bleaching bones" is a moot point. There is a primitive drawing on the wall of the Hava Supai canyon in Arizona which looks suspiciously like a dinosaur. This would mean that some of the great reptiles still existed after the advent of man.

In addition there is a provocative translation by Lieutenant Frank Hamilton Cushing of a Zuni Indian myth which runs as follows: *"They* were monsters and animals of prey. They were provided with claws and terrible teeth. A mountain lion was but a mole in comparison with them."

Occasionally there are tales of dinosaurish monsters still living in odd corners of the world, such as the jungles of Africa or South America. Unfortunately, however, I have yet to encounter one of these stories that had really good credentials. Some of them give you a feeling of fire behind the smoke, but you never quite see the fire.

For large dinosaurs to maintain themselves incognito on land would be a considerable undertaking. Not impossible, certainly, but still quite a job of hiding your light under a bushel.

On the other hand, for huge creatures from the age of reptiles to continue to exist in the depths of the sea is quite another matter. The seas of this earth are deep and broad, and we seldom see below the surface.

Dinosaurs had, as is shown by numerous fossil remains, several close relatives who inhabited the sea. These were of great size, had long sinuous necks, reptile-like heads, and were usually equipped with two sets of flippers.

Those who maintain that monsters from the dinosaur's time still survive in the sea point out that practically all accounts of sea serpents are rather accurate descriptions of prehistoric marine creatures. The bodies of such monsters probably would be largely submerged, only the peak of the back showing. This, seen in connection with the long curving neck, would give the impression of a giant snake.

When, on December 22, 1938, a trawler dredging off the tip of South Africa brought up a living lungfish, afterwards labeled *Latimeria,* which, by all rules of geology, should have been extinct for a hundred and thirty million years, the possibility of reptilian monsters surviving in the sea was given a great impetus.

So much for speculation. Now for some actual cases of "sea serpents" and/or sea-going dinosaur relatives. . .

AMONG the tales of monsters of the sea, that reported by those on board H. M. S. *Daedalus* is probably best known. For almost a century a storm of books, pamphlets, and articles has raged around the innocent head of that creature.

On August 6, 1848, the British corvette, *Daedalus,* was sailing in the south Atlantic at latitude 25° S., longitude 9° 37′ E. The weather was cloudy, but visibility good. At a little before five o'clock, a midshipman, Mr. Sartoris, sighted a peculiar creature swimming a few hundred yards from the ship and pointed it out to the officer of the watch, Lieutenant Edgar Drummond.

The report was then transmitted to Captain Peter M'Quhae. In the next five minutes the monster was observed through glasses by Captain M'Quhae, Master William Barrett, and three seamen.

The creature, according to Captain M'Quhae's official report, was ". . . an enormous serpent with head and shoulders about four feet above water . . . there were sixty feet of the animal above water . . . it's diameter was from fifteen to sixteen inches . . . its head without doubt that of a snake . . . It held on at a pace of from twelve to fifteen knots . . . passed so close under our lee quarter that, had it been a man of my acquaintance, I should have easily recognized his features with the naked eye."

Captain M'Quhae's report is in the files of the British Admiralty.

THE FOLLOWING tale comes from files of the British scientific journal, *Zoologist.* Henry Lee, formerly of the Brighton (England) Aquarium, elaborates the case in his *Sea Monsters,* published in 1883.

"Captain the Hon. George Hope states that when in H. M. S. *Fly* in the Gulf of California, the sea being perfectly calm, he saw at the bottom a large marine animal with the head and general figure of the alligator, except that *the neck was much longer, and that instead of legs the creature had four large flappers* . . .the creature was distinctly visible and all its movements could be observed with ease."

To anyone familiar with historical geology, it will be obvious that Captain Hope gave a good description of the pre-historic monster, *Plesiosaur*. Yet Captain Hope had never heard of either historical geology or the *Plesiosaur*. He merely recorded what he saw below the calm, transparent Lower California sea.

WHEN Major General H. C. Merriam, U.S.A., heard in 1903 that a party of ladies boating near Wood Island, Maine, claimed to have seen a sea serpent, he scoffed, a loud scoff befitting a Major General.

Two years later he was forced to withdraw said scoff. The method of withdrawal was a letter which he wrote to Dr. F. A. Lucas, American Museum of Natural History, New York.

General Merriam stated that about August 5, 1905, he was sailing off the Maine coast, opposite Wood Island Light, when his small pleasure boat was becalmed. Besides General Merriam, the boating party consisted of his sons, Captain H. M. Merriam, U. S. Artillery, and Charles Merriam, together with two friends of the younger men. The party decided to wait for a breeze, and were reclining on the cushions when:

". . . we were startled by a loud splashing in the water some distance off our stern, and looking in that direction, we saw what appeared to be a monster serpent. Its head was several feet above the surface of the water, its long body was plainly visible, slowly moving towards our boat by sinuous or snake-like motion.

". . . The animal continued its course, passing entirely around our boat . . . keeping a distance of about three hundred yards.

". . . it swam at a steady and rapid rate—not less than twelve miles an hour, keeping its head uniformly about four feet above the water and apparently intent upon examining our craft on all sides. It had no dorsal fin unless it was continuous.

"The color of its back appeared to be brown and mottled, shading down to a dull yellow on the belly. The head was like that of a snake, and that part shown above the surface—that is the neck—appeared to be about fifteen or eighteen inches in diameter.

". . . I estimated its length at sixty feet or more. During all the time occupied in swimming around us, which must have been at least ten minutes, the head remained uniformly above the surface of the water, and then it quietly dove and disappeared."

A few moments later a breeze came up and the party started slowly for shore. After they had sailed about a mile, their mysterious friend again appeared and swam parallel with the boat for some time before once more diving.

SOMETHING unbelievably monstrous, something with staring eyes a foot across, rose slowly out of the calm Pacific at eight o'clock of a September morning in 1920. At least that is the story as sportsman Ralph Bandini told it in *Esquire*, June, 1934. He said it was the sea monster of San Clemente, and that a hundred other men had seen it. A composite description of the creature had been sent to David Starr Jordan, president of Stanford University.

What Bandini claimed he saw was: a giant barrel shaped body which was six feet thick, topped by a reptilian head that was covered with thick, coarse hair. Widely spaced in the head were two bulging eyes at least twelve inches in diameter.

Obviously only a small part of the monster was above the surface. Bandini estimated that the bulk of the entire creature must have been greater than that of the largest whale. He mentions the odd fact that, although there was a little roll to the sea at the time, the monster did not rise or fall, as a whale would. The waves hit against it and broke.

Before the monster slipped again beneath the surface, Bandini's boat was less than three hundred yards from the creature. He was then observing it through seven-power binoculars.

Accompanying Bandini on the small power cruiser in which they had set out tuna fishing was a man named Smith Warren, well known in Southern California. He too saw the monster, his report agreeing with Bandini's.

The story is told first hand. It is of relatively recent date. Yet Bandini's monster is one of the most awesome.

Chapter 4

DAMNED SHIPS

MYSTERIES surrounding ships divide themselves naturally into three categories: ships which mysteriously disappeared, ships which, although in perfectly seaworthy condition, were found crewless, and that traditional specter, the phantom ship. I have included two stories of each type.

Until recent times, disappearance of ships was not particularly mysterious. Frail sailing craft, without wireless, were forever vanishing, victims of the manifold disasters which are the lot of those who struggle against the sea.

In this century there have been some peculiar disappearances, but although they are intriguing problems for speculation, theories involving the supernormal are not called for. In the two cases which I have described, the *Kobenhavn* and the *Waratah*, I have indicated the most logical of the explanations which have been offered.

I have not included the much discussed disappearance of the fuel ship, *Cyclops*, U.S.N., some time after March 4, 1918, on her way from Barbados to Hampton Roads, Virginia. Not only was the argument of a top heavy ship very strongly advanced in the *Cyclops* case, but the incident occurred in wartime when German submarines were active. This latter point seems to me a nearly fatal blow to the mystery.

Mysteriously deserted ships certainly pose many problems, but in most cases the explanation probably lies in murder, mutiny, and human aberrations. Men cooped up on small ships sometimes do strange things. Still, such cases are often baffling.

I have not included the mysterious abandonment of the *Marie Celeste*. That mystery has been written and rewritten so often that it is entitled to a little well deserved rest. Besides, the story with its ramifications is too complicated to be adequately presented in a book such as this.

The story of the phantom ship *Palatine* should be considered as an interesting and dramatic tale, rather than an factual account. I have never been able to find statements of witnesses who have seen the specter. However, it is fairly well established that some strange light—possibly of meteorological origin—is sometimes seen off Block Island.

The case of the spectral ship seen by British royalty is most puzzling. In describing the incident, the then Prince of Wales treats the matter with ultra-British matter-of-factness. It was just one of the experiences encountered during a long voyage. God in His infinite wisdom only knows what would have happened if a Frenchman had seen the phantom.

THE *Waratah*, a great new ship—her displacement was 16,800 tons—sailed on July 26, 1909, from Durban, Union of South Africa, bound for Capetown. Commissioned only a year before, she had already made two successful voyages from London to Australia. She was designed as a combination freight and passenger ship for the run around the Cape of Good Hope, a trip known for bad weather. After building, she was subjected to five different inspections, Lloyd's classifying her "100 A.1." She carried every known signaling and safety device—except wireless.

On July 27 she spoke the steamer, *Clan MacIntyre*. When she steamed out of sight of that ship, she might as well have steamed to the moon. There, on a well-traveled ocean, this large ship, brand new, carrying two-hundred and eleven persons, vanished.

Immediately following her disappearance, three warships and two privately chartered vessels searched for months. Not a bit of wreckage, not a board or a deck chair, life preserver or a human body, was ever discovered. When other great steamers have gone down, wreckage has been picked up for months afterwards.

Stranger still, the *Waratah* must have vanished within sight of land. Had any of her boats gotten away, they would have had a good chance of making the coast. If the disaster occurred at night, she could have signaled by blinker or rocket. But she didn't. She simply vanished.

Of the legion of theories advanced to explain her disappearance, the most credible has to do with her unusually heavy tophamper. The weather is known to have been stormy at the time she disappeared. If she were top heavy, she may have simply turned over in some great sea.

Yet she had made two voyages before without complaint by her officers, and was considered a reliable ship. The Court of Inquiry into the disaster concluded that she had "sufficient stability as laden." In any case, the fact that elaborate search conducted immediately after her disappearance revealed not the slightest trace of wreckage is certainly strange.

LARGEST and finest sailing vessel afloat, the five masted barque *Kobenhavn* slipped out of Montevideo harbor on December 15, 1928. She carried wireless and was equipped with diesel engines. On board her were sixty apprentices, young men from the best Danish families.

A few days later she was sighted off the River Plate. And then she vanished. Not one sound was ever heard from her wireless; not a splinter of wood identifiable with her, not a life boat, nor a spar was ever found.

The largest sailing ship afloat doesn't go down like a stone. A wooden ship may drift for years. And what of the silent wireless? and the diesel motors? and the apparent failure to lower a boat?

A year after the *Kobenhavn* disappeared, a missionary on the lonely island of Tristan da Cunha, stated that on January 21, 1929, he had seen a large and apparently derelict sailing ship drifting by at some distance from the island. Later it was discovered that a Finnish barque, the *Ponape*, had been sailing off Tristan da Cunha on the day that the missionary claimed to have seen the mysterious ship. The *Ponape* was in all probability what the good man saw.

Even if the derelict *Kobenhavn* was off the coast of Tristan da Cunha on January 22, and was unseen by the *Ponape*, why was no distress signal shown, no message from the wireless—and no boat lowered? If her engines and wireless were out of order, and her boats smashed beyond repair, why was no raft launched, no wreckage ever found?

ACROSS gray churning water, the master of the *Marathon* hailed the sailing ship *James Chester*. It was February

28, 1855, and the ships were in mid-Atlantic. The *James Chester's* rigging was tangled, and her decks were disordered; she refused to answer the *Marathon's* hail. Finally a boat was lowered, and the silent ship boarded.

The *James Chester* was searched from bow to rudder, but not a living thing was found. There was wild disorder everywhrere, but no hint of actual violence. No traces of blood, no weapons, no signs of struggle were found.

Although the ship's compass and papers were missing, *every boat was in place.* There was no lack of provisions or water. The ship was as sound as the day she was launched.

No trace of the crew was ever found. It is possible that there was an extra boat carried on deck, but even so, what dark terror would cause the crew to leave a staunch ship and put forth in one small boat when there was a thousand miles of storm-lashed water in every direction?

IN 1850, farmers and fishermen who inhabited a cluster of dwellings at Easton's Beach, near Newport, Rhode Island, saw a strange vessel making for shore. All her sails set and her flags snapping in the stiff breeze, she headed for the beach. A crowd gathered in expectation of the disaster when the vessel crashed on the shore.

But the ship struck the beach so gently that she came to rest uninjured. The crowd immediately boarded the vessel. She was the *Seabird,* under command of Captain John Huxham, and was expected that day in Newport on her return voyage from Honduras.

As the crowd clambered over the vessel, they found coffee boiling on the galley stove, breakfast laid out for the crew, charts and navigation instruments in order. But the only living thing on board was a mongrel dog, sitting quietly on deck.

An elaborate investigation failed to produce the slightest trace of the captain or the crew. Why, how, or where they vanished from a perfectly sound ship in calm weather, only God—and one mongrel dog—knew.

IF EVER a ship deserved a ghostly fate, it was the *Palatine.*

In 1752 she sailed from Holland for Philadelphia, crowded with immigrants. When supplies ran low, the crew mutinied and murdered the captain. Next the immigrants were starved and plundered.

Then with the ship leaking, the crew took to the boats, leaving the helpless *Palatine* to run aground in Christmas week off Block Island. There "wreckers" pounced on her, stripping her of everything left of value. They tried to sail the hulk, lost courage and cut her adrift—after setting her afire.

As the flaming ship drifted out to sea, she still carried one human being, a crazed woman who had refused to go ashore.

Through the years a tale emerged that on certain wild nights, a strange light—some said it was actually the phantom of the burning *Palatine*—could be seen off Block Island. In 1934 Edwin C. Hill, nationally known newspaperman, news reel editor, and radio commentator, investigated the matter. He stated in his *The Human Side of the News*:

"Hundreds have claimed to have seen the apparition, and the '*Palatine* light' is a well known phenomenon along the New England coast.

"*There is, apparently, some kind of light—strange, mysterious, inexplicable—which is seen far out at sea at certain times.*

". . . there are people living this day on Block Island who will tell you, with their hand on the Book, that they have gazed seaward in the blackness of the night, startled by a bright radiance at sea, and have watched, with straining eyes, while the *Palatine,* blazing from truck to keelson, swept along the horizon . . ."

ONE OF the witnesses of the following phantom was later King George V of England.

In 1881 Prince George of Wales was crusing on Her Majesty's Ship *Inconstant,* accompanied by his brother, Prince Albert Victor. At 4:00 A.M. on July 11, when the ship was enroute from Melbourne to Sydney, an eerie red light was seen off the port bow. What followed is vividly recorded in the Prince's diary, which was later published in the extensive work, *The Cruise of the Bacchante.*

"In the midst of the red light, the masts, spars, and sails of a brig two hundred yards distant stood out in strange relief as she came up. The lookout in the forecastle reported her as close to the port bow, while also the officer of the watch from the bridge clearly saw her. So did the quarterdeck midshipman, *who was sent forward at once to the forecastle; but on arriving, there was no vestige or sign of any material ship. The night was clear and the sea calm.*

"Thirteen persons altogether saw her. Two other ships of the squadron, the *Tourmaline* and the *Cleopatra,* who were sailing on our starboard bow, asked whether we had seen the strange red light."

In the record of men against the sea, this incident is certainly one of the queerest.

Chapter 5

GHOSTS

GHOSTS HAVE BEEN reported in all ages, and most ages have accepted them. If the truth were known, it is probable that the majority of persons now living believe in them. The number of words on the subject which have been printed, written, chiseled in stone, scratched on clay bricks, painted on papyrus, typed, engraved, and mimeographed is beyond the calculation of man.

Traditionally, a ghost is supposed to be a tenuous double possessed by men—and possibly by animals—which, under certain circumstances, becomes visible or audible. Occasionally it moves physical objects. It is usually assumed that this double survives death—at least for a time. Some careful investigators believe that ghosts have been photographed.

This chapter is not concerned with ghosts allegedly observed in connection with séances or similar gatherings. These might be designated as specially "called up" ghosts. The ghosts in this chapter are strictly spontaneous.

In an effort to select as varied stories as possible, I have taken the ghost conception in its broadest meaning. For instance, the story concerning Pavlova might equally well be classed as one of "possession." I have included animal ghosts, ghosts that were supposedly photographed, ghosts of persons who were not dead, etc.

The three chapters, "Ghosts," "Haunted Houses," and "Poltergeists" are of necessity interlocking and should be considered as a unit. Such phenomena are obviously connected, in at least a general way, with "Valley of the Shadow."

CRITICS HAVE declared that Maxo Vanka's paintings in the Croatian Catholic Church at Millvale, Pennsylvania, are "the best church murals in America." Certainly no murals were painted under stranger circumstances.

The project was so extensive that many artists might have considered a year as the minimum time for completing it. However, Rev. Albert Zagar, pastor of the church, was desperately anxious to have the murals finished in time for a mid-June celebration. This deadline allowed scarcely more than two months for the work. To speed up his work, Vanka painted every week day from morning until after midnight.

On the second or third night after beginning work, he was startled by a long drawn-out note which came from the organ at the rear of the church. The organ was electrically operated, and Vanka was surprised that it could spontaneously give forth such a powerful note.

On the fourth night Vanka was high on the scaffolding when he chanced to glance down and saw a dark robed figure gesticulating in front of the altar. The powerful floodlight which the painter used brightly illuminated the scene. Deciding that the figure was that of Reverend Zagar, Vanka went back to work. When next he glanced at the altar, the figure had gone.

The following night he again saw the figure, and went at once to ask Reverend Zagar about it. Vanka was at the time staying with the priest. When he entered the parish house, he found Father Zagar asleep in his chair. Usually, he was waiting for Vanka with a pot of coffee and a plate of cakes.

The priest said he had not been in the church. He also declared that the reason he regularly waited up for Vanka was a current story about a ghostly visitor to the church.

Father Zagar wished to be at hand should Vanka be frightened.

On a score of other nights Vanka saw the figure. Once the figure blew out the altar lamp, which was so protected that it could not be extinguished by any chance air current. *On another night, it lit a series of candles which continued to burn after the strange visitor had vanished.*

The figure was also seen by Father Zagar and by several other witnesses. Yet by Vanka's specific instructions, *the doors of the church were kept locked while he was working.* There were two keys. Father Zagar had one, Vanka the other.

Louis Adamic, author of *The Native's Return, My America,* etc., heard the story from Vanka. He carefully took down the painter's statement, then interviewed Father Zagar and other witnesses. He found that the identity of the spectral visitor had been the subject of much speculation in Millvale. However, he unearthed no significant facts on this angle of the case. The story most commonly accepted was that it was the ghost of a priest who had done certain things not strictly in keeping with the teachings of Jesus.

Adamic published a detailed report of the case in *Harper's Magazine,* April, 1938, from which source the above account is condensed.

No COLLECTION of ghost stories would be complete without tales of ghostly footsteps. The next two stories are of this variety . . .

It is said of Carolus Linnaeus (1707-1778), great Swedish scientist, that "He found biology a chaos; he left it a cosmos." Botany, too, owes a debt to Linnaeus' genius. At his death he left—along with his massive scientific works—a strange little manuscript in which he recorded a number of inexplicable personal experiences. Among them was the following:

On the night of July 12-13, 1765, his wife awakened him, saying that she had heard some one walking with a heavy step in Linnaeus' museum. Linnaeus also heard the footsteps. Identifying them as those of his old friend, Karl Clerk, he said to his wife, "I used to recognize Clerk, in Stockholm, merely by the sound of his footsteps."

But Clerk was not in Linnaeus' museum. In fact, there was no one in the museum. The single door to the room was locked and Linnaeus had the key in his bedroom. Nevertheless, he went down, unlocked his museum, and made a thorough search. There was not the slightest sign that anyone had been in the room.

A few days later, Linnaeus received word that his good friend, Karl Clerk, had died in Stockholm at precisely the hour his footsteps had been heard in the locked museum.

IF ANY ONE should have known whether the ghostly footfalls heard climbing the stairs of John Singer Sargent's studio in Tate street, London, were those of the dead artist, it would have been Alfred Orr. For many years Orr shared the same studio with Sargent. A few months after Sargent's death in 1925, Orr leased it.

All was quiet for over a year. Then Orr began to hear Sargent's characteristic footsteps. Orr's wife heard them. Visitors heard them. Orr declared:

"I'm not a spiritualist . . . but we've heard the footsteps so often . . . on the stairway, even in our bedroom. One night when I was in bed I heard Sargent's footsteps, then the bedroom doorknob turned all the way around and back again. We searched the house from top to bottom—nothing, as usual.

"Sometimes when I hear the footsteps I call, 'Come in, Pop!' We used to call him 'Pop' Sargent."

Orr's ghost story was picked up by the *Associated Press* and appeared in many American newspapers. Just a quiet tale by a responsible man about footsteps where there were no feet.

". . . WE THEREFORE commit this body to the deep, to be turned into corruption, looking for the resurrection of the body, when the sea shall give up her dead . . ."

There were two thin splashes in the quietly rolling Pacific. The traditional words for those who die at sea had been said. The bodies of seamen James Courtney and Michael Meehan had been dropped overboard from the tanker SS. *Watertown*, a vessel belonging to the Cities Service company. The matter should have been closed—at least until the ". . . resurrection of the body."

It was January, 1925, and the ship was heading for the Panama Canal. The men had been suffocated by gas fumes while cleaning a cargo tank.

A few days after the two men were buried, members of the Watertown's crew approached Captain Keith Tracy and explained a matter which much troubled them.

"Courtney and Meehan, Sir, they're following the ship. All of us have seen 'em. We see 'em every evening at twilight. They swim after the ship."

The Captain laughed. However, the reports persisted. Always the phantoms were seen off the side of the vessel from which the men had been buried. The heads would appear briefly, would often be seen by several men at once, then vanish. They seemed to follow the vessel.

The officers also saw them, and the Captain was sufficiently impressed to report the matter in detail to the officials of the company when he arrived in New Orleans. At the suggestion of James Patton, an officer of the company, the first mate of the Watertown secured a camera. Patton gave Captain Tracy a fresh roll of film, with instructions to keep it sealed and in his possession in case ghosts were again sighted.

Back through the Canal went the Watertown. As she neared the region in the Pacific where the seamen had been buried, there again were reports of ghostly things seen at twilight.

Late one afternoon the Captain took the mate's camera, broke the seal of the film, and himself loaded it. When the ghosts appeared, he made six exposures. The camera remained in the Captain's possession until the Watertown reached port.

A company official then took the film to a commercial photographer—who knew nothing of the strange story—and it was duly developed. Five of the negatives showed nothing unusual, *but on the sixth were what appeared to be images of two heads*. They were in the same position relative to the ship as when seen by the crew.

For some time an enlargement made from this negative was displayed in the offices of the Cities Service company at 70 Pine street, New York. The case was reported in *Fortune* magazine, also in a publication of the Cities Service company.

Later, Dr. Hereward Carrington, leading American investigator of psychic phenomena, interviewed officials of the Cities Service company. They verified the facts and showed him the photograph. He stated:

"There can be no doubt that at least one of the faces is a realistic portrait of the dead man."

The crew of the *Watertown* thought the photograph was a little superfluous. After all, they knew what they had seen.

I HAVE a spritely little case about the photographing of a ghost dog. It appeared, of all places, in a handbook on the care of dogs, *That Dog of Yours*, by Anne Elizabeth Blochin, published in 1941 by Macmillan Company of Canada, Ltd.

It seems that several hundred animal lovers had gathered for the ceremony of unveiling a central monument in a pet cemetery called "Happy Woodland." This cemetery was apparently located on property owned by the Blochins. During the ceremony, a visitor photographed a flower-banked grave marker. The visitor was interested only in the grave stone and saw no ghost, either human or canine.

As ghost photographs are always under suspicion, I simply quote Mrs. Blochin as to the denouement of the matter:

". . . On developing the negative, the photographer was amazed to see, clearly defined in the picture, the figure of a dog lying at the foot of the grave. She sent it to us with the query: 'Is this the spirit of your Happy Woodland?' It was the undeniable likeness of a dog, *though there were no living dogs in the cemetery at the time.*

"When the photograph was shown to the owners of the grave, they immediately recognized it as that of their pet, a beloved small mongrel . . . He had been buried there some months before. That this might not be thought the mere power of suggestion, they submitted several photographs of the dog in life, which show a resemblance so striking as to be remarkable."

In her book Mrs. Blochin includes excellent halftone reproductions of both the "ghost" photograph and a photograph of the living dog. I can vouch for the fact that in the reproduction at least the ghost photograph shows below the grave a very strong likeness of a dog's head and part of its body. There is certainly considerable resemblance between the ghost dog and the living animal.

IN THE same book Mrs. Blochin tells a most intriguing story concerning a ghost dog. The case is first hand.

A dog of hers, Solo, escaped from the kennel late one afternoon. Thinking Solo would soon return, the Blochin family sat down to their evening meal. A few minutes later the early evening train, which passed near the house, roared by. An instant later Mrs. Blochin saw Solo run past the dining room window. As he was close to the house, he was easily identified; she noted that he was running *away* from the railroad tracks.

The next morning Mrs. Blochin set out with another dog in search of the recalcitrant Solo. As she was passing through a wooded spot, Solo suddenly appeared. He trotted up to the other dog, and both wagged their tails, nuzzling each other. Solo was within a few feet of Mrs. Blochin, and there could be no possibility of a mistake in identification.

Turning towards home, Mrs. Blochin was surprised to discover that Solo had disappeared.

When she arrived at the house, her husband hesitantly informed her that Solo's body had just been discovered on the railroad tracks. The dog had apparently been killed by a train.

No train had passed since the one the evening before when the Blochins had been at dinner.

ALBERT PAYSON TERHUNE, dog expounder *par excellence,* considered the problem of ghost dogs in his *The Book of Sunnybank,* 1934, Harper and Brothers.

At one time Terhune had a big crossbred dog named Rex who was almost the size of a great Dane. Short-haired and fawn-colored, he had a jagged scar across his foreface. Rex spent his mortal existence following Terhune around.

Not being allowed in the dining room, the dog would usually observe the Terhune meals through the French windows just behind his master's chair. Rex had also chosen a spot in the hallway outside Terhune's study door as "his favorite and *only* resting place."

After Rex's death in March, 1916, his place was taken by a collie named Bruce. Hundreds of times Terhune called Bruce into his study, and invariably the dog detoured around the spot where Rex used to lie. His problems in avoiding this perfectly vacant spot were often comical.

In the summer of 1917, Terhune's lifelong friend, Rev. Appleton Grannis, came to Sunnybank after a long stay in the West. One hot afternoon he and Terhune sat talking in the dining room. As was his custom, Terhune's back was to the French doors.

Later, as they were leaving the room, Grannis remarked: "I thought I knew all your dogs. But there's one I never saw until now. The big dog with the short fawn-colored coat and a scar across his nose.

". . . this dog has been standing outside the window staring in at you all the time we were there. He's gone now. Which of your dogs is he?"

Reverend Grannis had never seen Rex, who had gone to his four-footed ancestors over a year before, nor had Terhune spoken of the dead dog to his friend. Terhune draws no conclusions. He merely cites the facts as he observed them.

THE NEXT two cases concern "ghosts" of men who weren't dead . . .

On Saturday, January 3, 1891, J. S. Thompson called at the photographic studio of James Dickinson, 43 Grainger street, Newcastle, England, and asked for a set of photographs which he had ordered. Dickinson told him that the photographs were not yet ready. Thompson seemed very disappointed, saying that he had little time left and could not return later for them. Then he walked out of the studio.

A large amount of painstaking research has gone into establishing those seemingly unimportant facts. The British Society for Psychical Research checked them. William Thomas Stead, editor of the *Review of Reviews,* thoroughly investigated them. The incident has been discussed in a score of more of books. But to the end, the facts have remained unshaken. Dickinson and the other witnesses swore that

Thompson had come for his pictures. The studio record book for that day showed a notation to the effect that Thompson had called.

On that Saturday morning of January 3, 1891, Thompson was actually at home in bed, under the constant observation of a nurse. During his delirium he mumbled continually about his photographs. But he never got them. For a few hours after *something* appeared in Dickinson's shop, Thompson, still muttering about his photographs, died.

AT LEAST one ghost has been reported seen during a session of the House of Commons. It was not, however, the ghost of a dead man. The affair appeared in the British press during May, 1905, and was analyzed by French astronomer and psychical researcher, Camille Flammarion.

A few days before the Easter Parliamentary recess in 1905, Major Sir Carne Rasch had a severe attack of influenza and was unable to attend a certain session of the House, although he desired intensely to support the government. At the height of the debate, Sir Gilbert Parker noticed Rasch seated near his usual place. A moment later Rasch disappeared.

Later two other members of the House, Sir Arthur Hayter and Sir Henry Bannerman, stated that they had also seen Rasch that evening seated on the bench he customarily occupied. Yet during the entire night of the debate, Rasch was tossing restlessly in his bed at home.

SO MUCH for ghosts of the living. The following story is more in the great tradition of ghost stories. I have yet to unearth an account of the incident actually written by Dr. Mitchell. However, it is apparent that he recounted the story many times. My specific source is naturalist George K. Cherrie, friend and co-explorer with Theodore Roosevelt. He gives the incident in his *Dark Trails, Adventures of a Naturalist.*

Hard driven snow hurtled across the streets of Philadelphia. It was early December and as night obliterated the washed-out daylight the wind rose to blizzard force.

Dr. S. Weir Mitchell, America's foremost neurologist during

the last quarter of the nineteenth century, had retired early. A long day with his patients had made a warm drink and his bed seem irresistible. Sleep was just snapping the last thread of consciousness when his door bell rang violently.

Struggling back to full awareness, Dr. Mitchell arose and answered the door. Standing in the whirling snow was a little girl, dressed in a cheap thin frock. About her shoulders was a ragged shawl.

"My mother is very sick," she declared, her voice flat in the cold. "Won't you come, please?"

Dr. Mitchell explained that he had already gone to bed. He suggested that there were many other good doctors nearby. He asked if the girl's family had no regular physician. The girl's only answer was: "Won't *you* come, please?"

Deep in Dr. Mitchell's mind a memory of the Hippocratic oath stirred restively. He asked the girl to step inside, and proceeded to dress. The girl said nothing more, but when the doctor had put on his great coat, she indicated that he was to follow her.

They walked through the whirling snow and entered a house. There the doctor found a woman desperately ill of pneumonia. The woman had once been a servant of the doctor. Strangely, the girl did not follow Dr. Mitchell into the sick room.

For a few minutes the doctor was busy examining the woman. When he had finished, he complimented her on the intelligence and persistence of her daughter.

The woman appeared bewildered. "But my daughter died a month ago. You will find her clothes in that little cupboard."

Opening the cupboard, Dr. Mitchell found the identical dress and shawl which the girl had been wearing. The clothes were warm. *They could not possibly have been out in that snow-filled night.*

That is the story as Dr. Mitchell, president of the Association of American Physicians, president of the American Neurological Association, holder of degrees from a dozen universities, often told it.

IT WAS 3:00 A.M. when "The Snowbird" ballet, based on the book by Lady Eleanor Smith, came to its final rehearsal. The audience in the darkened auditorium consisted of three people: Lady Smith, Charles Landstone, business manager for the production, and Henry Harrison, composer of the score.

The ballet had been inspired by the great Pavlova, who had died in 1931, but a few months before. In the climactic scene, the ballerina, Frances Doble, was to dance a routine similar to Pavlova's "The Swan."

As Miss Doble danced from the wings, those in the empty auditorium thought she appeared strangely small. As they watched, her figure changed, became in its every move and gesture that of Anna Pavlova.

Effortlessly as only Pavlova could dance, the figure went through the routine, but it was not the routine called for in the script—*it was Pavlova's routine.* To complete the dance, the figure, standing easily on one pointe, pirouetted three times—*a thing that Miss Doble could not do.*

The group in the theater hurriedly compared impressions. All three had seen the same thing. Their discussion was interrupted by Miss Doble, now standing in the wings. She said in a dull voice: "I am sorry—let's try it again. I couldn't dance. I must be awfully tired. My mind suddenly seemed to go blank."

She had no recollection of having danced the scene.

The incident as given above was recounted by eyewitness Lady Smith in her *Life's a Circus.*

Chapter 6

HAUNTED HOUSES

ALL HOUSES are probably haunted—haunted with the hope and fear, the hate, lust, and gallantry which their walls have enclosed. It has been suggested that this conception is more than figurative. This question, however, leads into the incense-scented dusk of mysticism.

Hauntings in this chapter are of a more robust nature. The phenomena which are alleged to have occurred are not merely

49

personal reactions to the "atmosphere" of a building. These houses were haunted in the sense that the average man understands the term.

The last case in the chapter I investigated myself. I am sorry that the persons involved remain anonymous. I believe anonymity to be seldom justified, and I discussed this point with the man in whose home the haunting occurred. I must say that his reasons for anonymity seemed intelligent and practical.

However, I can personally vouch for the case, and would be happy to furnish evidence to legitimate researchers in the field. I published a complete account in *Tomorrow* magazine, December, 1942.

Hauntings are of many kinds. Some seem purposeful, others merely casual. Sometimes a single building appears a focal point for a number of ghosts.

Accepting, for the sake of discussion, that haunted houses exist, certain interesting observations are worth mentioning.

One fact which has impressed many investigators is a sort of cycle in hauntings. Whatever force causes this type of phenomena seems to build up slowly and then discharge in an outburst of weird occurrences. The storing up process then begins again. However, this is not characteristic of all hauntings.

There is some evidence that the amount of static electricity present has an effect on the strength of the phenomena. The most powerful manifestations sometimes seem to occur during times of high static, such as thunder storms. This observation is traditional; however, it may also be entirely subjective.

At least two of the following cases are on the borderline between haunted houses and poltergeists, but the line of demarcation is vague at best.

Most hauntings seem to decrease in severity with the passage of years, and it is probable that no man's house will be eternally ghost-ridden.

BORLEY RECTORY, "most haunted house in England," is a charred ruin now. On February 27, 1939, a fire of mysterious origin destroyed a major part of the building. There are tales that phantoms still roam through the burned out rooms. But such specters are inconsequential—at least as far as scientific investigation of haunting goes. For by 1937 Borley Rectory had already been subjected to the greatest ghost hunt of modern times.

The Rectory, located in the hamlet of Borley, near Long Melford, Suffolk, England, has a lengthy reputation as a rendezvous for phantoms. A number of tenants, usually clergymen, were driven out by the manifestations. In 1937 the Rectory was vacant, and appeared likely to remain so.

On May 19, 1937, Harry Price, famous psychical researcher who had exposed scores of hauntings, leased the Rectory for a year. To make his investigations as unbiased as possible, he advertised in the newspapers for sceptical-minded persons willing to spend time at the Rectory and report anything that occurred. He finally chose a staff of forty observers who kept almost constant watch at Borley.

Written instructions as to the technique of scientific observation were given the observers, and each turned in a report after every period spent at Borley. *Almost every observer reported strange occurrences.*

Lights were seen at windows, raps and footsteps heard, objects were thrown about and mysteriously moved. A special electrical contact installed by the investigators was pressed *in a vacant and sealed room*. Both dark and luminous figures were observed.

Messages were mysteriously written on the walls. In one case the same area of the wall was photographed at one hour periods. During one interval, fresh marks, which showed clearly on the second film, had been added. The room had been sealed and guarded during the time between the two photographs.

British philosopher Dr. C. E. M. Joad reviewed the case in *Harper's Magazine*. He felt that it was necessary to postulate that some supernormal agency—*or agencies*—was active in the building.

Price was also convinced that the phenomena were genuine, but he was never able to find any satisfying pattern or purpose in the hauntings. He thought that the haunting was probably multiple. His elaborate account of the investigation, *The Most Haunted House in England,* was published in 1940.

If you are interested in haunted houses in general—and the scientific investigation of phantoms in particular—read his book. It is indeed worthwhile.

IN THE STAID *Atlantic Monthly*, June, 1942, may be found the record of a queer little incident from the darker side of things. The story is told by renowned British writer, Robert Graves.

During the winter of 1919-20, Graves spent some time in an ancient stone house named Maesyneuadd, near Talsarnau, North Wales. The building was supposed to be haunted, and on several occasions Graves saw doors suddenly open, apparently moved by a supernormal force. Once he observed a lamp shade jump straight off the lamp.

On New Year's Eve of 1919 Graves was present at a gathering around the drawing room fireplace. The group was drinking mulled claret. Just before the year died, Graves set his glass on a side table at the corner of the fireplace.

When, two or three minutes later, he again reached for the glass, it had been drained dry. No one had entered or left the room—*in fact no one had moved from the semi-circle of chairs, and no one except Graves could have reached the glass without taking several steps.*

It is a simple little incident, but all hauntings need not be tumultuous.

WHAT FORCE transported moths into a closed steel and concrete room, then five minutes later caused them to vanish, is something of a problem. The incident was part of a series of inexplicable occurrences which in 1934 ruined the vacation of an American university professor.

The account of the haunting was published in *Harper's Magazine*, November, 1934, under the title, "Four Months in a Haunted House"; the author's name was given as Harlan Jacobs, but the article carried the following editorial notation:

"*The name signed to this article is not the author's real name. He occupies, however, an important position in one of our leading universities. This is a veracious account of actual experiences . . . The Editors.*"

Harper's is one of the most meticulously reliable magazines in the United States. The article is written with great sincerity and elaborate detail. The author is obviously a man of high education and scientific training. Therefore, the fact of anonymity—usually fatal in cases such as this—does not seem significant.

The haunted house was a small summer cottage on Cape Cod. When Jacobs rented it for the summer, it had been built nine years before, but for some unstated reason had never been occupied.

For such a house to be haunted breaks all tradition. Haunted houses should have a background of bloodshed, rape, and murder.

While the Jacobs occupied the cottage, some "force" rapped, clicked, banged, made sounds like "a sheet of newspaper that swished across the floor," "a matchbox falling from the dresser," and "a rolling pin rolling across the floor." An inexplicable light was once seen in one of the bedrooms. Concerning each of the above mentioned phenomena, Jacobs goes into long paragraphs describing his efforts to find a normal explanation.

A concrete and steel garage, which had been sealed shut for months, was mysteriously filled with hundreds of moths. Five minutes after the moths had been discovered, the garage was again visited, and not a single insect could be found. The garage had been tightly closed between the two visits.

The only thing traditional about the haunting was ghostly footsteps. "I am not speaking of any muffled sounds . . . I am speaking of a steady tramp, tramp, tramp, as of a person with good leather heels walking . . ."

The most startling phenomenon was a resounding crash which occurred periodically, sounding like "a grand piano falling off its legs."

Besides Jacobs and his wife, the phenomena were observed by several visitors. The case is solid—and utterly unromantic.

I HAVE several times set fine strings across the stairs at various heights before going to bed, after all the others have gone up to their rooms. *I have at least twice seen the figure pass through the cords, leaving them intact."*

That was one of the scientific observations made by Rose C. Morton during the investigation of "The Lady in Black," who haunted Bognor House in England. As the case is presented, the name "Bognor" may be fictitious. The evidence was published in the *Proceedings of the British Society for Psychical Research,* Vol. VIII, 311-32.

Miss Morton was a medical student when her family moved into Bognor House. The house had been built in 1860, and the Mortons arrived in March, 1882. "The Lady in Black" was often seen between 1882 and 1889. Miss Morton prepared a careful and highly scientific report of the case. Her report was supplemented by signed statements of six other witnesses.

The haunting was quiet, almost prim. The phantom was seen quietly wandering around the house. On several occasions Miss Morton tried to speak to her, but she appeared not to hear. If the ghost were cornered, she simply disappeared.

Occasionally light footfalls, such as a small woman would make, were heard. Sometimes the figure was seen in an orchard near the house.

The reaction of the family's dog was noted: ". . . Twice I remember seeing our dog run up to the mat at the foot of the stairs, wagging its tail and moving its back the way dogs do when they are expecting to be caressed. It jumped up, fawning as it would if a person were standing there, but suddenly slunk away with its tail between its legs. . . . Its actions were peculiar and were much more striking to the onlooker than it could possibly appear from a description."

The reporting of the case was painstaking, the ghost refined. Perhaps she was just a quiet English woman unaware that she was dead.

THE NEXT STORY might be called "The Case of the Phantom Barkeep." At any rate, the ghost seemed to have more humor than most of his tribe.

This is the case, mentioned in the introduction, which I personally investigated. The man in whose house the occurrence took place is a professor in one of America's five largest universities. A major part of his work is in evaluating facts. He has spent his life learning how to determine what is true.

The story is recounted from stenographer's notes taken at the time of the interview. The man is in his late thirties. Here is the story—much compressed—as he told it:

The family rented a house in San Francisco early in 1933. The previous tenants had left suddenly, after staying only two months. Before that time the house had been occupied by one family for twenty years.

Almost from the day the professor arrived, footsteps were heard on the basement stairs. He stated positively that there was no point in blaming the footsteps on mice, rats, or creaks in the framework of the house. *They were footsteps.* Distinct heel and toe action was heard. In general, the footsteps were *louder* than those of average persons.

Night after night, the man assembled a group of friends and waited for the footsteps. One person would stand beside the basement door, another by the light switch. When the footsteps began, the light would be turned on and the door opened. Always the stairs were vacant.

Once his wife, while washing dishes, placed her rings beside the sink. With the washing done, she reached for the rings. They had vanished. An elaborate search finally discovered them in a high cupboard that could be reached only with the help of a stepladder.

They lay on a thick layer of dust. The dust was undisturbed. Only by the use of the stepladder and elaborate precautions could the rings have been laid in that position without marking the dust.

There were a number of other phenomena, such as the mysterious movement of a very heavy chair—at times when it was certain that no one was in the room. The rest of the story I give in the professor's words:

"The only other member of my family, our two-and-a-half year old son, could have had no part in the phenomena. He had barely begun to talk and was too young to conceive and carry out such pranks—*moreover, on many occasions he was under observation when phenomena took place.*

"His only contribution to the mystery was an enigmatic one. Several times my wife entered his room to see how he was sleeping, only to find him wide awake. He always explained that:

" 'I was talking to the old man who comes to see me every night.'

"Often my wife questioned him as to what the man said. The answer was usually confused, but it boiled down to: 'We talk about this house and wheels.'

"The strangest, most dramatic, and best attested of our ghost's enterprises concerns an ordinary bitters bottle. I have thought over that incident countless times during the last few years. I have questioned and requestioned the witnesses, and I just can't find a *normal* explanation.

"I kept our liquor and mixing ingredients in a very high cupboard. Only a tall man—I am just over six feet—could reach it. The kitchen is very large; the butler's pantry is at the far end, at least twelve feet from the liquor cupboard.

"On the evening in question I was about to mix the first drink for a party. I took down a handful of bottles from the shelf and carried them into the butler's pantry. When I reached the pantry, I realized I had neglected to bring the bitters.

" 'Damn it,' I said, 'I've forgotten the angostura.'

"No one was in the kitchen. Four guests were near me in the pantry. *No one was within ten feet of the liquor cupboard.*

"I had hardly finished my expression of disgust, when something fell at my feet. *It was the bitters bottle, unbroken.*

"Here are the plain facts:

"The bitters bottle *might* have rolled out of the cupboard, although it was at the back. But in that case it would have fallen *directly below* the cupboard. *Five* witnesses besides myself saw it fall *from the air* beside me, *twelve feet* from the cupboard. It fell with a very definite thud.

"We spent the next hour thumping on the sides of the cupboard with our fists and a hammer, trying to make the bottle come out. It wouldn't even fall out, let alone *fly* out."

Perhaps never in the history of haunting has a phantom performed so useful a task.

Chapter 7

POLTERGEISTS

POLTERGEISTS may have tremendous significance, but they are usually insufferably dull. Granting that the phenomena are genuine—psychical researchers accept them, orthodox psychologists deny them—the supernormal powers behave like stupid clowns.

The word "poltergeist" is German and means literally "noisy ghost." However, the real poltergeist specialty is throwing things, particularly rocks or objects of furniture. Sometimes, the objects appear to materialize out of space, at others they are simply moved within a room or a house.

Let me make it clear that I am not endeavoring to sell the case for the poltergeist, nor am I necessarily stating my personal belief in the matter. I am merely attempting to give a very brief background to an extremely complicated subject.

Poltergeistic phenomena of great violence are sometimes reported. Furniture and other objects are apparently thrown at living persons. However, instances of persons being actually injured are rare.

Poltergeists have been reported in all ages and from all parts of the world. In 1935 Dr. Hereward Carrington collected three hundred and eighteen cases from thirty-three countries. I briefly note three cases which occurred during recent years near my home in Southern California.

Stones, heavy walnuts, and bones thrown upon the home of E. H. Burdette, Fresno, California. Police struck by the missiles. No solution. Dispatch over *United Press*.

Nails, pieces of tile, and small images mysteriously dropping into small print shop near Los Angeles City Hall. Shop was operated by Mr. and Mrs. Harry Park. Occurrence reported, with pictures, in *Los Angeles Herald*, July 12, 1939.

Los Angeles Times and *Herald*, January 5, 1943—A girl, 13, named Norma Moore, was focal point for unaccountable disturbances. She moved from Ventura, California, to Los Angeles, but the phenomena followed her. Occurrences witnessed by her adult relatives. Objects thrown about, water glass smashed against a wall, unexplained sounds, etc., etc.

So it goes . . . In many cases poltergeistic force seems to be intimately connected with a living person, often a boy or a girl at puberty. This has led to speculation that the power may be connected in some inexplicable way with maturing sex. However, the theory that an adolescent is *necessary* for poltergeistic phenomena has now fallen into disrepute.

At times it has been proved that children perpetrated the disturbances as pranks or to gain attention, but the number of cases in which such an explanation has been established is relatively small.

Charles Fort once expounded the theory that deluges of objects falling on a small area originated somewhere in space, and were not terrestrial phenomena at all. Later he seems to have changed horses and tended towards the poltergeist theory.

It remains that, if poltergeistic phenomena have actually occurred, objects have been moved by an unknown force and matter has been passed through matter. Philosophically, such occurrences would be more world shaking than the atomic bomb.

The three cases included in this chapter show the wide variety of manifestations attributed to poltergeists. I do not claim that they are "typical," but I hope they are intriguing.

In 1922, rocks began falling from the sky in a certain section of the town of Chico, California. The area affected was approximately the size of a city block. The rocks were oval, varying in weight from an ounce to over a pound. They always fell straight down.

By March, the "Chico Miracle" had spread from the local papers to the national press associations. On March 16, there was a particularly heavy fall of "warm" rocks. On the 17th, a deluge of the stones descended upon a crowd, injuring one person.

The police of Chico searched for blocks around the affected area. They found nothing. They stationed guards around the accursed spot. The rocks still fell. Professor C. K. Studley, from a local college, investigated. He reported in the *San Francisco Examiner* that "the larger rocks . . . *could not have been thrown by ordinary means.*"

Police Marshal J. A. Peck of Chico spent two full months investigating the phenomena. In the end he gave up, saying, "I could find no one who could explain the matter. Many times I have heard and seen the stones."

A few months later the falling stones stopped of their own accord. And the "Miracle of Chico," defying months of investigation, passed from the headlines, still unexplained.

ABOUT a small burial vault in Barbados "considerable ink has been spilled." What went on within this ill-famed sepulcher has been the subject of a number of investigations.

British man of letters Andrew Lang discussed the case at length in the *Folk-Lore Journal*, December, 1907. Lieutenant Commander Rupert T. Gould, R.N., gave the matter a full going over in his *Oddities*. There have been a number of other accounts, beginning with a record of the occurrences written by Rev. Thomas H. Orderson, who was rector of Christ Church where the vault was located.

In 1807 the first coffin was placed in the vault. From that date to early in 1812, the vault was twice opened and other coffins placed in it. When the vault was once more opened, late in 1812, several of the huge lead-lined coffins were found thrown about. The caskets were straightened, and the vault closed with a stone slab which required six men to move.

Twice again the vault was opened to receive additional coffins. Both times the coffins already in the vault were found scattered in confusion. Each time things were again put in order.

The whole matter did not square well with the normal sunlit world of rationality. It was said, with considerable justification, that dark powers were involved.

Finally, Lord Combermere, Governor of Barbados, decided to put a stop to the nonsense. On July 17, 1819 the body of one Thomazina Clarke was placed in the vault. Lord Combermere was present at the burial. He was a hard bitten soldier, who, but for a bit of politics, would have led the British Cavalry at Waterloo. People, he thought, had a right to peaceful sleep in British ground.

He had the walls of the vault sounded, the floor covered with sand, and the only opening sealed. A guard was placed before the sealed entrance.

When the vault was next opened on April 18, 1820, in Lord Combermere's presence, the coffins were once more found in a heap. *The seal had not been broken. There were no footmarks in the sand.* That was enough for His Lordship.

The vault was left empty, it being deemed unsuitable for eternal rest.

PIERRE VAN PAASSEN relates the following incident in his best seller, *Days of Our Years*. It is one of the weirdest supernormal occurrences of modern times, yet it seems necessary to either accept it on its face value or call van Paassen an out-and-out liar.

During the winter of 1929, when van Paassen was living in Bourg-en-Forêt, France, he saw a black dog pass him on the stairs. The house was searched, but no dog found. The following night the dog was seen again.

Van Paassen then left on a trip to Roumania, and on returning, found his household greatly excited. Several persons had seen the mysterious dog. Van Paassen, together with a neighbor, Monsieur Grèvecoeur, and Grèvecoeur's son, kept watch the following night. The dog duly appeared at the head of the stairs. Grèvecoeur whistled. The dog wagged his tail. All three men ran forward. As they did so, the outline of the animal grew fainter, and it vanished.

Two evenings later van Paassen, with his two police dogs beside him, waited for the phantom. It appeared at the usual hour, came halfway down the stairs, and again faded away. A moment later both his dogs seemed to be struggling with some invisible adversary. Then one dog fell dead. Investigation showed no external injury.

Van Paassen then called a priest, the Abbé de la Roudaire, who waited with him the following night.

When the dog appeared, the priest looked straight at the

apparition; then he took a step forward. The dog gave a low growl. Then its outline became hazy, and it vanished.

Silently, the priest led the way back to van Paassen's study. There he asked:

"You have a young girl in your house, fourteen—fifteen?"

"Yes, Monsieur l'Abbé. We have a girl who runs errands. She is fifteen, I think."

"Pay her a month's wages and let her go!"

"You do not mean this girl has anything to do with the apparition?"

"Such instances of poltergeists," the Abbé said slowly, "frequently center around a girl in puberty. But it is the first time I have seen it take the shape of a dog . . . There is nothing to worry about now. You should have called me before."

The dog was never seen again.

Chapter 8

FORGOTTEN EXPERIMENTS

CERTAIN experiments seem born under a dark star. When they are first announced, they appear of great importance, but nothing more is ever heard of them. They are never finally proved or disproved, but seem doomed, like the "Flying Dutchman," never to reach port.

There are many reasons why experiments receive no better fate than to be "forgotten." Their results may be grimly at odds with the established beliefs of the time. The experimenter may step on some one's toes, or he may run out of money; he may become irascible and a recluse, or he may die.

In this chapter I have used the word "experiment" in its broadest possible meaning. I have even stretched it to cover "research" and "investigation." In this way I have been able to include several cases which, although they were not strictly experiments, seemed more at home here than in any other chapter.

Although but a handful are presented here, forgotten experiments are legion.

FOR MANY YEARS, Jules Romains, renowned French writer and philosopher, conducted experiments in an effort to prove his strange hypothesis *that human beings can see through their skin.* Having observed several cases of supernormal sight, Romains came to the conclusion that, as the human eye had evolved from skin tissue, the epidermal cells still had the latent ability to transmit visual impressions.

Romains elaborated this theory in his *Eyeless Sight.* He believed that Ranvier's manisci, microscopic nerve organs of the skin, are potential eyes, and claimed that, under his training, blind subjects learned to distinguish light and dark with "eyes" in their cheeks, fingers, and noses. He stated that some of his subjects were able to read type, to distinguish colors.

He believed that his experiments explained cases of so-called "x-ray eyes," of people who had driven cars blindfolded, and the natives of Samoa who claimed that the blind can see through their flesh.

On Christmas Eve, 1922, Romains gave a remarkable demonstration. Three subjects were blindfolded by an oculist in the following manner:

Strips of adhesive tape were placed in the form of a cross over the eyelids. This was covered by two rectangular pieces of black silk. Finally, a bandage consisting of black plush, with oval pads for the eyes, was fastened in place.

Blindfolded in this manner, the subjects were given photographic printing frames which contained letters, numbers, and colored pieces of paper covered by glass. By placing the frames near their foreheads or fingertips, the subjects were able to distinguish blue, red, and green colored slips of paper, make out numbers such as 380, 20, 4, etc. They also could "see" the general outlines of simple pictures.

Among the eminent men who attested the validity of the experiments were M. Ledoux-Lebard, R. Maublanc, Dr. B. L. Couchoud, Dr. Charles Robert, and Anatole France.

IMPOSSIBLE—Yet It Happened!

In 1927, after many experiments, Sir Jagadis Chunder Bose, world renowned horticulturist, concluded that plants have a nervous system similar to animals. With delicate instruments he claimed to have detected the reaction of plants to pain, to have recorded their heart beats.

He tested plants with poisons, found they reacted in the same way as animals. Ether and chloroform made them unresponsive to electrical stimuli. In death, garden peas liberated charges of electricity.

A resume of Sir Bose's experiments was published in the *Literary Digest*, September 17, 1927. His discoveries—if substantiated—would appear of the greatest significance to horticulture.

At six o'clock on a March evening in 1933 an earthquake rocked Southern California, left over a hundred dead. The center of the damage was the town of Compton. *Seismographs placed the center of the quake thirty miles away, under the town of Newport.* Newport wasn't damaged.

But the fallen tombstones didn't agree with the seismographs. They placed the center of the quake directly under the center of damage, which seemed more logical. That was as Dr. Thomas Clements of the University of Southern California had expected.

Dr. Clements had conducted experiments in upsetting stone markers by means of artificial earthquake shocks and had come to the conclusion that, by plotting the direction of fall of such markers, the center of a quake could be told much more accurately than by seismographs.

He suggested that his experiments could be checked at the time of earthquakes by noting in what direction tombstones fell. In fact, Dr. Clements checked his theory himself—in the Helena, Southern California, and Santa Barbara quakes. He tied his experiments in with those conducted by Japanese geologist Omori, who worked with stone lanterns.

If Dr. Clements' conclusions were proved accurate, an important new light would be thrown on earthquake phenomena. It was in 1936 that the tombstone investigation was last heard from.

SOME OF my researches indicate that plants may give forth a strange radiation," said Moscow horticulturist Dr. Alexander Gurwitsch. "Why not an experiment . . . ?"

Working at the Histological Institute of the First Soviet University, he selected a symmetrical onion root, and encased it in a metal tube, so that it looked like a tiny cannon with the tip of the root protruding at the firing end.

Then he chose a second root and also covered it with metal, except for a small area on one side. Next he directed the tip of the "sending" root at this uncovered spot on the "receiving" root. The exposure was for three hours. Later, microscopic examination showed that cell growth in the area exposed to the root cannon had been greatly speeded.

There was a long song and dance about Gurwitsch's work in an article, "Radiation and Life, *Harper's Magazine,* July, 1934. It stated that he was still at work on the problem.

JUST BEFORE World War I, science decided to test once and for all the supposedly mythical abilities of "diviners" who found water with forked sticks.

An outstanding investigator was selected. He was Professor W. F. Barrett, then holding the Chair of Experimental Physics in the Royal College of Science for Ireland. His investigations covered many months, a large number of outstanding diviners being tested. Summing up his findings, Professor Barrett stated:

"At first sight few subjects appear to be so utterly beneath scientific investigation as the divining rod. Nevertheless . . . my careful and critical examination shows that certain diviners have a genuine facility or faculty for finding underground water. *This faculty no known scientific explanation can account for.* Personally, I believe the explanation will be found in some faculty akin to clairvoyance."

His conclusions were startling and disturbing. Scientists seldom refer to his investigations. Water diviners go on finding water with forked sticks.

THE NEXT time I feel a pain in my arm, I will note the time. Then, perhaps, I can prove something."

So spoke Frederick George Lee, regular blood donor of the Middlesex Hospital, London, who believed he felt a pain in his arm each time a person to whom he had given blood died.

When next he felt such a pain, he carefully noted the time, then checked it against hospital records. It was the exact moment when the person to whom he had last given blood had died.

Twenty-four times in three years Lee gave blood at the Middlesex Hospital. Seven of the patients died. Seven times Lee felt:

". . . a severe pain in his arm at the precise moment of the patient's passing. He was depressed, distressed, and overcome with illness every time.

"Remarkable, because in no case did Lee behold the patient during the transfusion, in no case was he aware of the patient's condition until the last moment came with its twinge for his arm."

Those are the facts of the "strangest experiment in telepathy" as given in *Time* magazine, September 7, 1925. From the context it is apparent that Lee was still serving as blood donor for the Middlesex Hospital when the *Time* item was written.

In 1920 Dr. W. J. Kilner published a work, *The Human Atmosphere,* describing certain experiments through which he claimed to have discovered a shell of radiation surrounding the human body. He called this radiation the "human aura."

His investigation began in 1908, when he was connected with St. Thomas Hospital in London. While conducting certain experiments, he chanced to employ a viewing screen stained with a little-used dye, *dicyanin.* By viewing a nude human being through this screen, he discovered that he could see a distinct cloud of radiations extending for about eight inches around the body. These radiations often showed varying colors. At death the "aura" disappeared.

Dr. Kilner claimed that when any part of the body was seriously diseased, the aura around it showed marked changes. Utilizing this discovery, he made many diagnoses.

Shortly after he first reported his findings, several scientists, among them Dr. C. Martin, and Dr. Barker Smith, corroborated his findings. Havelock Ellis stated that, by using Dr. Kilner's screen, he could easily see the "aura."

Dr. Kilner was not a mystic. He thought he had made a contribution to the science of diagnosis. Perhaps he had. Perhaps his experiments might become the basis of a fundamental advance in medicine. Perhaps he was a deluded fool, playing with a pretty blue dye. Who knows?

LAZARUS III returned to some semblance of life on Friday, April 13, 1934. On May 19 this revivified dog was able to walk and eat regularly. On June 4 he and the man who had raised him from the dead were requested to vacate the laboratory at the University of California.

Dr. Robert Cornish killed Lazarus III, who was one of a series of experimental dogs, by asphyxiation with nitrogen. After four minutes of death, the dog was brought back to life by a technique which, in a cruder form, had been partially successful when tried on other canines. The brains of these dogs had not fully recovered, and they had eventually died a second death.

The method of revivification combined artificial respiration by means of a special apparatus, and an injection developed by Dr. Cornish. The injection contained blood from another dog, heparin, a physiological salt solution, epinephrin, and gum arabic.

Certainly Dr. Cornish's experiments were some of the most promising conducted in revivification. Dr. Cornish considered his work only begun. The last heard of it was an item stating that Lazarus III had been alive three months, and was apparently regaining his faculties. That was in July, 1934.

It is possible that some day a vote of thanks may be in order for Lazarus III, and posthumous citations for Lazaruses I and II.

Chapter 9

ENIGMAS OUT OF SPACE

IF LIFE exists only on this earth, then perhaps the gods are really dead, and creation but an idiot's tale. This is for man ultimate loneliness. For, if in his tinkering with atoms or other toys, he succeeds in destroying all life on the earth, he thereby destroys all life that is, and bequeaths a dead universe to the dead gods.

But there are those who have dreamed that life exists on other worlds. Many have tried to prove this, usually by hypothesis or analogy, occasionally by facts.

It must be admitted that there have been some startling astronomical observations. And there are certain other data which whisper that in the bleak void of space there are other islands where life has found a home. Strange tales of things beyond our planet have been told, and forgotten, since the days of the Chaldeans—or earlier.

Modern speculation about extra-terrestrial life centers around three themes:

A. That primitive living matter—or fossil remains—have fallen on the earth. I have presented two cases bearing on this point. Both of these cases, i.e., the investigations of Drs. Lipman and Hahn, have been heavily attacked, and are certainly not conclusive. I have included short summaries of the arguments against them.

B. That certain observations of the planets—and even the moon—indicate the presence of life; that there is evidence in some cases that this life is conscious, and that it may have attempted to communicate with the earth. The background of this ancient debate is far too vast to be reviewed here. The evidence, both pro and con, is massive.

C. That conscious beings from other worlds have actually reached this earth and navigated our skies in space ships. This is a most astounding theory—there

are other words for it. It was a favorite of Charles Fort.
Certainly there have been authentic reports of queer
things seen in our skies. They may have been of meteorological origin, or they may not. I merely present them.

When the United States Army dreams of a rocket to the
moon in our time, and hopeful pioneers claim that all the
fundamental problems of space travel have been solved, the
doings of fellow travelers—if any—in our universe are certainly worth consideration.

BITTER AND LONG has been the argument as to
whether life could have reached the earth by means of mete-
orities, and thereby begun the process of evolution which
produced a two legged, perverse creature called man.

In 1932 Dr. Charles B. Lipman of the University of California conducted some direct experiments on the subject.
His method was to soak meteorites in antiseptics, flame them
with burning alcohol, then finely grind material from their
centers. Next the meteorite particles were dropped into sterile flasks containing proper media.

Bacteria grew in the flasks. Some of the organisms were
autotrophic (requiring neither organic carbon nor organic
nitrogen). Lipman claimed that the bacteria could only have
come from inside the meteorites, where they had remained
dormant during the trip through outer space.

Between 1933 and 1935 Sharat Kumar Roy, assistant
curator of geology at the Field Museum, Chicago, repeated
Dr. Lipman's experiments. Bacteria also grew in some of
Roy's flasks. He thought the weight of evidence was that
these bacteria had been picked up during the laboratory
processing of the meteorite.

He therefore attacked Lipman's conclusions on the basis
of contamination from earthly sources, and on several other
grounds. Lipman still asserted that his bacteria probably
came from the depths of space.

IF FOSSILS were found in meteorites, it would prove
that far advanced life existed elsewhere in the universe. Ac-

cording to German geologist Dr. Otto Hahn, he found fossils in meteorites. This was in 1880.

The fossils Dr. Hahn claimed to have discovered were those of corals, and in some cases showed whole branches of animal formations. He published an illustrated monograph describing his discovery. The fossils were later examined by Dr. D. F. Weinlander, a competent zoologist. He agreed that they were undoubtedly the remains of living creatures.

Most of the meteorite fragments from which Dr. Hahn recovered the fossils were from a single fall in Knyahinya, Hungary. In describing the discovery in *Popular Science* it was suggested that all the fragments came from a "single extra terrestrial body which seems to have been overtaken by a great catastrophe."

Apparently Dr. Hahn believed he had unearthed fragmentary evidence of the death of a world—a world on which life existed. He published photomicrographs of thin sections of his meteorites. Several investigators, particularly British student of meteorites Dr. L. Fletcher, thought that Dr. Hahn's fossils were really *chondrules*, elaborate crystalline formations having no connection with living organisms.

THERE IS on the moon a jagged, sun-blasted crater which bears the noble name Plato. This crater appears no different from the others on our pock-marked satellite. But for over a century there have been whispers of strange doings in and around Plato.

In the years 1783 and 1787 Sir William Herschel reported seeing lights on that region of the moon. In 1847 Rankin claimed to have seen luminous points during an eclipse. Four other instances of lights were reported during the next few years. A fantastic observation was made of lights "that looked like torches of a procession."

In 1923 Flammarion speculated that "the variations [in surface coloring] actually observed even prove that the moon is not altogether a dead world." The color variations are particularly marked around Plato.

And in 1937 Professor William H. Pickering, one of America's leading astronomers, stated that "there are reasons for believing that there is life on the moon." His observations applied particularly to the region near the same crater.

The British Astronomical Association Journal for 1938 contains a report by Robert Barker concerning some color changes which he observed in the region of Plato. On December 12, 1937, he was examining this crater, using a four hundred and twenty-power eyepiece.

He observed a streak of orange-brown, intensely colored, which stretched along the crater's west wall. A review of Barker's report was published in the American magazine, *Rockets,* for May, 1945. This review was written by R. S. Richardson, and I quote therefrom:

"He describes the colored band as not an unbroken patch or layer, but as composed of many veinings or thin streaks, closely interwoven. Four hours later an irregular extension was seen spreading westward down the wall.

"He observed the same colored area again on January 16, 1938, and on the following night found it had overflowed the wall to the floor, so that it was no longer a streak but an irregular varied surface of color.

"*In Mr. Barker's opinion, the area is exactly like a quick growing vegetation, which has fourteen and three-quarters days in which to complete a cycle of germination, growth and fructification.* He admits that many readers will probably consider his observations as fantastic, but nevertheless he is prepared to risk such criticism."

THE NIGHT of December 7, 1900, was far from uneventful on the planet Mars—according to astronomer Dr. Percival Lowell. On that night the Lowell Observatory at Flagstaff, Arizona, saw a shaft of light project outwards from the disk of Mars. The brilliant beam appeared to be hundreds of miles in length. It was observed for seventy minutes.

The light seemed to fluctuate. Dr. Lowell even thought he could distinguish some sort of code. However, he was never able to translate the code into a meaningful message.

The phenomenon was given world wide publicity. Professor William H. Pickering said the occurrence was "absolutely inexplicable."

THERE WAS once a gigantic cross on the disk of Mars, according to Giovanni Virginio Schiaparelli, director of the observatory at Milan. The cross was light colored, and was centered in a dark circle whose diameter was approximately nine hundred miles. A few months later he stated that the cross "had been removed."

To the day of his death in 1910, he maintained that he had seen the cross and that it was carefully centered in the dark circle. To the day of his death he also maintained that he had seen "canals." Modern telescopes and cameras have proved that he *did* see a network of lines which he called "canals." (Whether these apparently straight lines indicate the work of intelligent beings remains a moot question.) Perhaps Schiaparelli's observation of the cross was also valid.

If we, reasoning beings on the earth, considered sending a message across space, a message using the simplest type of symbol to prove that there was conscious life on this planet, what symbol would we use? It might well be a light cross on a dark field—a cross later removed to indicate that it was placed there only as a signal.

I do not have the date of Schiaparelli's observation, but it is recorded in *Major Mysteries of Science,* by H. Gordon Garbedian, 1933.

ON SEPTEMBER 2, 1921, a radio technician of some small renown named William Marconi declared that he was now convinced that he had received radio communication from some station not of this planet. The messages, which he had picked up on his yacht, *Elektra,* were of a wave length ten times that produced by any station on this world. This convinced Marconi they could not be of earthly origin.

In the *New York Times,* September 2, 1921, J. H. C. Macbeth, London manager of the Marconi Wireless Telegraph Company, Ltd., outlined Marconi's views. The dispatch reads, in part:

"Marconi could not accept the atmospheric or electrical disturbance theory because his signals were intercepeted regularly regardless of other interferences.

". . . Until Marconi conducted his experiments on his

yacht . . . radio receiving apparatus was capable of receiving wavelengths up to 24,000 meters. His receiving apparatus was tuned to many times this figure. With this he picked up waves estimated at 150,000 meters, and their regularity disproved any belief that they were caused by electrical disturbances.

"The only resemblance to the code used on this planet is in the letter 'V' of the International code. These 'V' operations were conducted time after time, much after the manner of station calls or test signals sent out from radio stations."

Marconi did not say that the messages were from Mars. He merely said that they were messages on a wave length which no station on the planet Earth could produce, and that they appeared to form some type of code.

ON THE NIGHT of August 22-23, 1924, Mars swung nearer the earth than it will be again in this century. The distance between it and the earth was approximately thirty-four and a half million miles. And during that time of nearest approach, all radio stations on earth were silenced for five minutes out of every hour.

The earth was waiting for a possible radio message from the Red Planet. Dr. David Todd, professor emeritus of astronomy at Amherst College, organized an international network of listening posts. At Dr. Todd's suggestion, the United States Government, through diplomatic channels, requested countries having high-powered transmitters to silence them for five minutes out of each hour. In 1924 the number of high-powered transmitters was relatively small.

At Washington, D.C., Dr. Todd made arrangements to have any incoming signals recorded photographically. An inventor, C. Francis Jenkins, had just perfected what he called a "radio photo message continuous transmission machine." This device automatically recorded incoming messages on a roll of photographic film. The film slowly wound through the machine, and signals were impressed on it by light flashes.

Between 7:30 and 10:00 P.M. on the night of August 22, R. I. Potelle, chief engineer of station WOR, Newark, New Jersey, heard strange signals. He reported the following day that the signals were repeated many times, and were a series of dots and dashes that belonged to no standard code. Other stations corroborated his report.

Meanwhile, in Washington, the film continued to move through Jenkins' complicated machine. At the end of the twenty-four hours of Mars' nearest approach, the film was removed from the machine and developed. On August 27, Dr. Todd called in reporters and described the results of his experiments.

The film showed two separate series of dots and dashes. Neither corresponded to any known code. U. S. Army code experts puzzled over the film, but came to no conclusion. Eventually, a copy of it was sent to the Radio Division of the U. S. Bureau of Standards, where it probably still is.

Mars swung back into space, the mystery surrounding it only deeper.

As a SPECIAL feature, the editors of *Observatory* invited astronomer E. W. Maunder to contribute some reminiscences to the five hundredth number of their magazine. The reminiscences were duly contributed. They concerned a strange celestial object seen November 17, 1882, by Maunder and his colleagues at the Royal Observatory in Greenwich.

The peculiar object appeared suddenly and moved steadily across the sky. It was observed with a large telescope. Concerning it, Maunder and his colleagues made numerous notes. Here are a few:

"The thing was cigar shaped—like a torpedo, a spindle, a shuttle—had the incident occurred a third of a century later, it would have been called 'like a zeppelin'—too fast for a cloud, too slow for a meteor—appeared to be a definite body—had a dark nucleus—extraordinary and alarming."

There was an aurora that evening, but not particularly brilliant. Maunder states positively that the strange thing in the sky had nothing to do with the aurora phenomena.

THE BRITISH SHIP, H.M.S. *Caroline,* was steaming slowly through the East China Sea, between Shanghai and Japan, on the night of February 24, 1893. At 10:00 P.M. some "unusual lights" were reported to Captain Charles J. Norcock. He went on deck to investigate.

The lights were clearly visible between the ship and the shadowy mass of the coastline. At that point the land rose six thousand feet, and the lights were below the summit of this mountain.

There were several lights, appearing to have a globular shape. Sometimes they moved together as a mass, then they would string out in a line. Finally, after having been under observation for two hours, they bore northward until they were lost to sight.

The following night the lights were again visible. This time they were in sight for seven hours. They proceeded at approximately the same speed as the *Caroline*. For a time they were eclipsed by a small island. Captain Norcock observed them through a telescope. With this he could make out that they were reddish and seemed to emit a faint smoke. Moreover, *they cast a reflection on the water below them.*

Captain Norcock states that in the same locality and at about the same time, Captain Castle of H.M.S. *Leander,* saw similar lights. Captain Castle altered course and made towards them. The lights moved away as if they were trying to evade the ship.

Captain Norcock made a full report of the affair, which was published in *Nature,* May 25, 1893.

That was ten years before the Wright brothers made their famous experiment at Kittyhawk, and in so doing inaugurated heavier-than-air flight. In 1893 balloons were in use, but it is extremely doubtful that any man-made lighter-than-air contrivance was traveling above the lonely China Sea on that February night.

A STRANGE procession of unknown things was seen in the sky on February 9, 1913, according to reports gathered by astronomer Professor Chant of Toronto, and published in the *Journal of the Royal Astronomical Society of Canada.* Professor Chant's collection of observations covered numerous points in northern United States and Canada.

Early in the evening of February 9, a luminous body was seen near the horizon. Soon it began traveling in a straight line across the sky. It was observed that ". . . the body was composed of three or four parts, with a tail to each part." This group, or complex structure, moved with a "peculiar majestic deliberation. It disappeared in the distance, and another group emerged from its place of origin." A third group followed.

According to another observer, "there were probably thirty or thirty-two bodies, and the peculiar thing about them was their moving in fours and threes and twos, abreast of one another; and so perfect was the lining up that you would have thought it was an aerial fleet maneuvering after rigid drilling."

Meteors are not supposed to move slowly and horizontally across the sky, nor in orderly fashion. Airplanes were in their infancy in 1913, but no one ever suggested that they were the cause of the inexplicable lights. In such matters one man's guess is as good as another's.

Chapter 10

POSSESSORS OF STRANGE POWERS

THIS CHAPTER contains stories of a number of persons who seem to have had abnormal powers. Some of them possessed their strange abilities for most of their lives, others were gifted for only brief periods; sometimes the power would come and go, fitfully.

Powers of many kinds are described—the power to find hidden water and the power to stay afloat indefinitely. It is possible that all these miraculous talents are but different outlets for a single unsuspected well of human power. There are those who have maintained this. But at the present status of man's understanding of these matters, such philosophical hypotheses tend more to confuse than enlighten.

Therefore, the following stories are presented as isolated cases, little islands of inexplicable data. No attempt is made to weave their complex threads into a meaningful pattern.

Almost all of the persons who appear in this chapter were outstanding figures in their day. They were not only abnormals—they were famous abnormals. How many thousands of obscure people have possessed similar powers is, of course, impossible to say.

I was somewhat hesitant over including the story of D. D. Home in this chapter. He was once the focal point of the three-cornered debate betwen materialism, spiritualism, and orthodox religion. Personally he took little part in the argument, allowing others to judge the significance of his powers. As far as religion goes, he died with a Greek Orthodox priest in attendance.

He was a celebrated figure in the courts of Europe, a worldly man, cultured. Whatever he did was on a grand scale. No cult, religion, or philosophy now uses his case as a key point in the argument as to human survival of bodily death.

He remains a strange figure. He was a man who seemed posessed of weird powers, a maker of magic. As such he is included in this chapter.

WHATEVER was the secret of "the man they couldn't drown," he carried it with him to his grave. He died peaceably August 2, 1931, in Jacksonville, Florida. It would have been luscious irony if he had died in water, but it was not so.

The basic facts of the case were published in a *New York Herald Tribune* obituary for August 13, 1931:

"Angelo Faticoni, known as 'The Human Cork,' because he could stay afloat in water for fifteen hours with twenty pounds of lead tied to his ankles, died . . . He was seventy-two years old.

"Faticoni could sleep in water, roll up into a ball, or assume any position asked of him. Once he was sewn into a bag and then thrown head foremost into the water, with a twenty-pound cannon ball lashed to his legs. His head reappeared on the surface soon afterwards, and he remained motionless for eight hours . . .

"Some years ago he went to Harvard to perform for the students and faculty. He had been examined by medical authorities who failed to find support for their theory that he was able to float for such great lengths by the nature of his internal organs.

"Faticoni had often promised to reveal his secret, but he never did."

AT SIX o'clock on a summer evening in 1759, Emanuel Swedenborg, world renowned scientist and philosopher, said to a friend whom he was visiting in Gottenburg that there was a great fire burning in Stockholm. He stated that the house of a mutual acquaintance was being destroyed.

At eight o'clock of the same evening Swedenborg declared that the fire had been stopped only three doors from his own house.

It is three hundred miles from Gottenburg to Stockholm. At that date, in mid-eighteenth century, there seemed no normal means by which the news of the fire could have reached Swedenborg. Yet, even to the most minute detail, the fire occurred exactly as he described it.

The facts of the case were recorded at the time, and are excellently attested. They may be found in any standard work on Swedenborg.

Such displays of apparently supernormal power were common in the life of Swedenborg. Incidentally, he has been made the central figure of a religion, which bears his name.

John Wesley, founder of Methodism, once received the following letter from Swedenborg:

"February, 1772

"Sir: I have been informed by the world of spirits that you have a strong desire to converse with me. I should be happy to see you, if you will favor me with a visit. I am, Sir, your humble servant."

Wesley read the letter in the presence of some of his preachers, one of whom, Rev. Samuel Smith, recorded the incident. Wesley informed the group frankly that he had been very strongly impressed with a desire to see and converse with Swedenborg, and that he had never mentioned the desire to anyone.

In reply to Swedenborg's letter, Wesley wrote that he certainly desired to meet him, but, owing to previous commitments, could not do so for six months.

Swedenborg replied that Wesley's proposed date would be too late, because he, Swedenborg, would go into the world of spirits on the 29th day of the next month.

Swedenborg died of palsy, but in complete possession of his faculties, March 29, 1772.

LATE IN 1917 when the sands of Wilhelm's Germany had almost run out, German military intelligence did a strange thing. It assigned one Dr. Franz J. Polgar to the job of interviewing captured allied officers—*because of apparently irrefutable proof that he could read men's thoughts.*

Dr. Polgar, a Hungarian lieutenant, had been knocked unconscious by the explosion of a hand grenade in a dugout. On regaining consciousness, he discovered that he had acquired an uncanny ability to read the thoughts of people around him. In the hospital he constantly told doctors and nurses exactly what they were thinking—sometimes with uncomplimentary results. His weird faculty was duly reported to the German Intelligence.

The Germans never succeeded in exploiting Polgar's powers. One reason for this was that Polgar became increasingly bitter against the Kaiser's military machine. After the war, he went to America.

On May 1, 1936, before psychologists from New York University, Dr. Polgar—one time pupil of Sigmund Freud—obeyed *mental* commands. Without a word being spoken, he took off a man's vest and placed it on a girl. That was the act on which the savants had been concentrating.

The scientists suspected simple explanations, particularly subconscious whispering by those present, combined with abnormal hearing by Dr. Polgar.

Another experiment was conducted in a small room—with only scientists present. One psychologist concentrated on a certain series of actions. He told no one. In fact, he didn't open his mouth.

Dr. Polgar was brought in. At once he went to a microscope, and from the table beside it he took a folder, opened it, and removed a piece of paper. The psychologist said nothing. Five times Dr. Polgar repeated the same procedure. At last he said:

"I cannot get away from the folder."

The psychologist admitted that Dr. Polgar had performed exactly the actions he had concentrated on, that he had remained silent in an attempt to confuse the mind reader.

Psychologists tried other tests. Polgar passed them. He discovered mentally the details of a faked murder, which had been planned as a test. One of the investigators merely concentrated on the details of the imaginary crime.

On May 2, the *New York World-Telegram* carried a long article on Dr. Polgar, written by the paper's science editor. It was headed:

"SKEPTICS YIELD ON THOUGHT TRANSFERENCE."

WATER DIVINERS are many (see the investigation by Professor W. F. Barret described in "Forgotten Experiments"). I have selected Kelly as representative of his species because of the dramatic circumstances under which his witching took place.

In the fall of 1917 General Allenby's British forces were attacking Turkish troops before Jerusalem. Allenby's troubles were many—and greatest of all was the lack of water. In the desperate situation somebody thought of an Australian soldier named Stephen Kelly who was supposed to be fey in such matters. He was asked if he thought he could be of assistance.

"Yes," Kelly replied. "I can find water. You see, I'm a diviner."

Kelly looked over the ground around the sun scorched desert outpost of Abu Ghalyan. He looked also at the two bone dry holes where British engineers had tried to find water. Then he went to work. "Dig here," he said.

Abundant water was found at thirteen feet. And with their water supply secure, the British columns moved on—on across Palestine to destroy the Turkish army and take Jerusalem.

The world well remembers how General Allenby dismounted and entered Jerusalem on foot. The world has long forgotten the water diviner named Kelly without whom it is doubtful whether Allenby would have reached Jerusalem at all.

LUTHER BURBANK, horticultural genius of our time, scorned all things supernormal—yet he wrote the following statement:

"I inherited my mother's ability to send and receive telepathic communications. So did one of my sisters. In tests *before representatives of the University of California* she was able, seven times out of ten, to receive messages sent to her telepathically.

"My mother was in poor health during the last years of her life. During these years I often wished to summon my sister. On such occasions I never wrote, telephoned, or telegraphed her. Instead, I sent messages telepathically. Each time she arrived at my home in Santa Rosa, California, on the next train."

When Burbank died in 1926 the eulogies were many and wordy, but no one mentioned that little investigation at the University of California—nor the mystery of the genius who used telepathy as practically as most of us use the telephone.

THOMAS A. EDISON was another outspoken sceptic, but at least once in his lifetime the great inventor admitted that he had witnessed an utterly inexplicable demonstration. He reported the incident in *Annales des Sciences Psychiques*, 1915.

To test the clairvoyant faculty of a famous wonder worker named Bert Reese, Edison performed the following experiment:

Reese was seated in one room while Edison went to another quite a distance away. There he wrote on a slip of paper: "Is there anything better than hydroxide of nickel for an alkaline electric battery?"

As Edison entered the room where Reese was waiting, Reese said: "There is nothing better than hydroxide of nickel for an alkaline electric battery."

Edison ruled out coincidence. Fraud seemed impossible. To the end of his life he was never able to explain the incident.

ANNA MONARO, asthma patient in the Pirano, Italy, Hospital slept fitfully. Three eminent professors, Fabio Vitali, G. C. Trabacchi, and Sante de Sanctis, sat watching her.

Suddenly a wisp of blue light, a flickering uneartly flame, glowed on the woman's breast. It faded, brightened, faded again. The scientists bent close. They agreed that the flame *cast no shadow*.

For days the professors had been aranging this test. The woman and her bed had been searched, the room examined.

The strange glow which flickered on Signora Monaro's breast had first been noticed by hospital attendants. Sceptical doctors, who had once laughed at this inexplicable occurrence, also believed that they saw the strange light.

Even under test conditions so severe that fraud seemed utterly impossible, the light was seen on a number of occasions by several witnesses. However, attempts to photograph it were complete failures. The affair occurred in 1934, and the professors above mentioned published a full report of the matter under the title *Sul Fenomeno di Pirano*, Rome, 1934.

IT IS difficult, if not impossible, to find a parallel to the career of that arch psychic, Daniel Douglas Home. This is particularly striking in view of the fact that not once was he "exposed."

Home was born in Edinburgh, Scotland, in 1833, and before he died at Auteuil, France, June 21, 1886, he succeeded in astounding two continents. Princess Metternich once said that Home had transformed the Tuileries into a "regular witches' sabbath."

Recently the fantastic story of Home's life has again attracted public attention through the publication of the best seller, *Heyday of a Wizard*, by Jean Burton in 1944. This is an excellent biography of Home.

Leaving aside the spiritualistic implications of Home's feats, he was noted for three types of miracles: his ability to touch and handle fire with impunity, levitation (the inexplicable rising and floating of his body), and the mysterious movement of heavy objects. The following is typical of the first of these strange powers:

In 1867, when Home was thirty-four, he met young Lord Adare, British war correspondent for the *Daily Telegraph.* Along with several other witnesses, Lord Adare saw Home stir the embers in a fireplace to a flame with his hand, then "kneeling down, place his face among the burning coals, moving it about as though bathing in water." His face was then examined. There were no indications of even singeing.

On the same evening Home picked up a glowing coal and carried it about in his hands for several minutes. The coal remained so hot that no one present could bear it closer than four or five inches.

Home's friends and supporters included Napoleon III, the Empress Eugenie, Count Alexis Tolstoy, Elizabeth Barrett Browning, Thackeray. Rare were the famous of the period who had no experience with him.

Thomas Adolphus Trollope, brother of the novelist Anthony, once consulted the most famous stage magician of the time, one Bartolomeo Bosco. Bosco laughed at the idea of trickery in Home's performances. He declared Home's miracles were beyond anything known to any mere conjuror. Elizabeth Barrett Browning wrote that ". . . everybody is quarreling with everybody on the subject."

In New York Dr. Robert Hare, professor emeritus of chemistry at the University of Pennsylyania, tried to discuss his experiments with Home at the American Association for the Advancement of Science, but was shouted down.

Home's miracles were never performed on a stage. Generally, they took place in the homes of friends, usually people of distinction. He never accepted money for his demonstrations.

Yet on scores of occasions he apparently rose into the air and floated about. Those present often passed their hands around him while he was suspended in mid-air. He once rose straight upward until he could make a chalk mark on the ceiling of a high room.

On another occasion he is supposed to have floated out one window, seventy feet above the ground, and back in another window. This affair was described in detail in three separate written accounts of the witnesses.

Heavy pieces of furniture, which would take several men to carry, were often moved by an unseen force—although Home at the time was separated from them by many feet. His exploits are too varied to permit detailed accounts here. Concerning the phenomena, Home himself said:

"I have not, and never had, the slightest power over these manifestations, either to bring them on, or to send them away, or to increase or to lessen them. What may be the peculiar laws under which they have become developed in my person, I know no more than others."

In 1870 there was a popular clamor for a formal investigation of Home. The man chosen for this job was William Crookes (later Sir), a brilliant young—he was thirty-eight—physicist and chemist. Crookes (inventor of the x-ray tube which bears his name), must inevitably be classed as of the very great of British science.

In investigating Home, Crookes used a considerable amount of apparatus, much of which he had specially designed for the experiments. He reported his results in the July 1, 1871, issue of the *Quarterly Journal of Science.*

He stated that, under conditions of perfect control, Home had floated in the air supported by an unknown force, and had handled red hot coals without injury. Objects in Home's vicinity had been moved by an unknown force.

Because of that report Crookes carried to the grave the stigma of having once been a fool and a dupe. Yet he never changed his mind. Twenty years later he wrote:

". . . I find nothing to retract or to alter. I have discovered no flaw in the experiments then made, or in the reasoning I based on them."

Let it be noted to the eternal shame of the Royal Society, of which Crookes was a Fellow, that not a single member would even attend one of Crookes' experiments with Home.

BEFORE one hundred fifty physicians gathered on May 2, 1936, for the express purpose of exposing him, Pat Marquis, twelve-year-old Los Angeles boy, *apparently saw without eyes.*

Blindfolded by three eminent eye specialists (Drs. A. G. Hovde, Henry S. Nesburn, and Lloyd Burrows), the boy duplicated gestures made by the doctors, took a book from the shelf and opened it to the page asked for, read tiny letters engraved on a watch fob, and correctly worked a ouija board no matter in what position the board was placed.

To make a foolproof blindfold, dark glasses were covered with adhesive tape; more tape was used to fasten the glasses to the boy's face. In all, three layers of tape, extending down to the upper lip, were used. A heavy dark bandage was used as a final covering.

The boy passed every test the doctors could devise. He acted exactly as if he had normal vision. Under the precautions, trickery seemed about as easy as stealing the Pacific ocean. The doctors finally admitted that the boy had "supernormal sight and cognition."

The investigation of Marquis was reported in a long illustrated article, *Los Angeles Times*, May 3, 1936.

Although the points of dissimilarity are many, it is interesting to compare this case with the theory of "eyeless sight" advanced by Jules Romains (see "Forgotten Experiments").

THE STORY of Mollie Fancher, although almost forgotten, has lost nothing of its mystery. Among the possessors of strange power, she is outstanding.

In 1866 Miss Fancher passed into a mysterious trance-like condition. Her physician, Dr. Samuel Fleet Speir, declared that for years her body had the cold of death, her breathing practically stopped, her pulse became almost indistinguishable. *During a period of nine years she consumed less food than a normal woman would eat in forty-eight hours.*

Noted specialists were unable to explain her living death—but when she returned to consciousness, they were faced with even a greater mystery. Now she seemed endowed with supernormal powers. She could distinguish colors in total darkness, could describe the dress and activities of persons hundreds of miles away. She could read unopened books and letters which were placed beneath her bed clothing.

On one occasion Dr. Speir brought with him an unopened letter which he had received that morning. While he held it, still sealed, in his hand, Miss Fancher wrote out its contents word for word.

There was no dark hocus pocus about Miss Fancher's case. The scientists who investigated her were free to apply whatever tests they wished. Among those who certified her supernormal powers were famed neurologist Dr. Robert Ormiston, Dr. Willard Parker, and Dr. Parkhurst, great astronomer of his time.

On February 3, 1916, having spent fifty years in bed and violated half the laws of science, she invited President Wilson to attend her birthday party. The President refused. Eight days later she was dead.

Chapter 11

HOUDINI

HARRY HOUDINI seems almost to belong in the last chapter. Yet there is something about the man and his doings which resents classification. I have therefore dealt with him separately.

Houdini's career, with its overtones, is in a sense a single complicated mystery. As he became more and more a legend, many of the facts surrounding him tended to be forgotten or distorted. Not only is Houdini a legend, he is also a symbol, a symbol of the sweetly restful conception that all miracles can be simply explained by the expert conjuror.

Something is marvelous and inexplicable. So what? Houdini did better—and he did it by trickery. The hand is quicker than the eye. Miracles of all ages are but rabbits from an empty hat.

Unfortunately, there are a number of incidents connected with Houdini's own life which cannot be so simply explained. He claimed that all of his feats were performed by simple mechanical trickery. Perhaps they were. Yet mysteries gathered around him like small boys around an unattended football.

A few of these incidents I include in this chapter. There were many others.

His long association, ending acrimoniously, with Conan Doyle, is a masterpiece of befuddlement on both sides. The details give you the feeling that each felt the other had too good a case.

Houdini died hard. Riddled with peritonitis, beyond the hope of medicine, doomed, he remained alive day after day. To his incredulous physicians, this was a minor miracle. Finally he said, "I have fought this thing—but I'm tired." He died October 31, 1926—on Halloween.

He was buried in a special metal coffin—in which he had been buried before. He had once spent an hour in it under water to duplicate the performance of another wonder-worker, Rahman Bey.

Showman he lived, showman he died.

SEVERAL YEARS before his death Houdini told Sir Arthur Conan Doyle that he would give him final proof that trickery could produce marvels which would put spirits to shame. But what was actually proved is hard to say.

The persons present at the test—conducted at Houdini's home—were Houdini, Conan Doyle, and Bernard M. L. Ernst, President of the Parent Assembly of the Society of American Magicians. A carefully examined slate was hung by Conan Doyle in the middle of the room. Five plain cork balls were examined, and one, picked at random, was cut open. It proved to be solid cork.

Another ball was then placed in a pot of white ink. Conan Doyle was next asked to walk anywhere he chose and write a sentence on a piece of his note paper.

Doyle walked three blocks, turned a corner, and wrote on a paper which he shielded in the palm of his hand. Meanwhile Ernst stayed with Houdini to see that he did not leave the house. After he had finished writing, Conan Doyle folded the paper and placed it in an inside coat pocket. Then he returned to the room where Ernst and Houdini were waiting.

Next Houdini told Conan Doyle to pick up the ink soaked cork ball and press it against the slate. This was done.

The ball stuck to the slate, then began to roll over the surface. As it rolled, it wrote the Biblical phrase "*Mene mene tekel upharsin.*"

That was the message which Conan Doyle had written on the slip of paper in his coat pocket.

When the writing was finished, the ball fell to the floor. Conan Doyle picked it up and took it home, along with the four unused balls. Upon examination, they all proved to be solid cork.

Houdini said he did all this by trickery. Doyle declared Houdini must have been aided by psychic power. Houdini still refused to explain how it was done. Ernst, a top flight magician himself, was completely mystified. Doyle reminded Houdini that he had once given up a mind reading stunt because he did things that even to himself "seemed spooky."

Ernst then begged Houdini—for the good of his crusade against spiritualism—to reveal the secret of the cork ball trick to either himself or Doyle—*in the strictest confidence*. Still Houdini refused.

Houdini never used the trick, if trick it was, on the stage. To the day of his death he never explained it. After nearly twenty years Ernst has been unable to concoct a satisfactory explanation.

During the time when Houdini conducted an active campaign against fraud and trickery in spiritualism and the supernatural, he kept a vast file of reports on his investigations. At his death, many of these reports came into the possesion of Joseph Dunninger, great conjuror and mystifier himself.

In this voluminous material there was the record of one case which baffled Houdini. His handwritten record was carefully preserved in a separate file. It is given below:

"Los Angeles, April 11, 1923. Having been approached . . . in reference to photographs to be taken of Mrs. Mary Fairfield McVickers who, before she passed away, requested that photographs should be taken over her body at five o'clock in the afternoon of the day of her funeral, saying that she would appear in spirit form, I . . . got in touch with Larry Semon [movie producer] to let me have a camera man . . .

"At 3:45 Nathan B. Moss of the Keystone Press Illustration Service, Los Angeles, walked in with his camera and plateholders loaded with fourteen negatives. He had no idea what I wanted . . .

"We went to Howland and Dewey, Kodak representatives, for a dozen 5 x 7 . . . The clerk pulled out five packages . . . I laid them on the counter before a gentleman whom I had never seen, asking him to select one, which he did . . . I personally handled the package, walked into the darkroom with Moss. He took out his own plates, and as he handed them to me, the plates just purchased were loaded into the plateholders.

"He then placed all the loaded plates in his regulation grip . . . On arrival at the church we took ten exposures . . .

"When we returned to the Chamber of Commerce building, we entered the darkroom, and in my presence the plates were developed immediately, *and on one we beheld a peculiar streak*. Mr. Moss made a print from this plate which caused a great deal of talk.

"*Not one photographer could explain how this could be tricked*. Mr. Moss offered a hundred dollars to anyone who could produce it under the same conditions, whereas no one could duplicate it. Signed: Houdini."

Dunninger published Houdini's notes in his brochure, *Houdini's Spirit Exposés*, 1928. Dunninger stated that Houdini *offered a thousand dollars* to any stage magician who could duplicate the effect under similar conditions. The offer was never accepted.

A reproduction of the photograph in Dunninger's brochure shows the "streak" as a heavy band of light with a globe or ball of luminescence at one end. The nature of the peculiar marking is such that it would be practically impossible for it to have been caused by a defective plate, plateholder, or camera.

Houdini, himself an expert photographer, noted the baffling incident in his diary: "Took pictures at church. A peculiar test."

But it was around Houdini's own death that the greatest storm of argument raged.

It is widely believed that Mrs. Houdini denied steadfastly that she ever received the prearranged "death message" from her husband, the message which was to prove that Houdini had mastered the lock of the door that baffles all men.

If it were true that Beatrice Houdini had always denied

receiving the message, the matter would be simple. But the actual facts of the case form a riddle worthy of the Sphinx. Perhaps solving the mystery of death is more complicated than picking a lock.

Some time before the magician's death, Houdini and his wife arranged a secret message which the first to die was to endeavor to transmit to the other. The message was to be delivered in code. Several persons were familiar with the code, *but the message itself was known only to Houdini and* his wife.

Shortly after Houdini's death, his wife offered $10,000 to anyone who could give her the prearranged message. A year later Mrs. Houdini withdrew the offer. On January 8, 1929, *after the offer had been withdrawn,* a psychic, one Rev. Arthur Ford, gave her a message which she at once recognized. Two days later she prepared a statement for the press. She was certainly definite:

"Regardless of any statements made to the contrary, I wish to declare that the message in its entirety, and in the agreed upon sequence, given to me by Arthur Ford, is the correct message prearranged between Mr. Houdini and myself. Beatrice Houdini."

Later, she apparently believed a rumor existed that she had faked the message incident as a publicity stunt. She therefore wrote to Walter Winchell, then on the staff of the *New York Graphic:*

"This letter is not for publicity. I do not need publicity. I want to let Houdini's old friends know that I did not betray his trust . . . Now regarding the séance. For two years I have been praying to receive the message from my husband. For two years every day I have received messages from all parts of the world. Had I wanted a publicity stunt, I no doubt could have chosen any of these sensational messages . . .

"When the real message, *the* message that Houdini and I had agreed upon came to me and I accepted it as truth, I was greeted with jeers . . .

". . . My husband made it possible for me to live in

the greatest comfort. I don't need to earn money. *I have gotten the message that I have been waiting for from my beloved, how, if not by spiritual aid, I do not know.*

". . . In conclusion may I say that God and Houdini and I know that I did not betray my trust. For the rest of the world I really ought not to care a hang, but somehow I do. Therefore this letter . . .

Sincerely yours,
"Beatrice Houdini"

And then her faith seemed to grow thin. She began to wonder if the message were conclusive. Yet to the end of her life she never denied that the message was the correct one.

On July 22, 1935, she stated in the *Los Angeles Examiner*: "I receive many messages that are supposed to come from Houdini through mediums and strange séances, but they never mean anything to me. Very often I go to séances, hoping and praying that the signals Houdini gave me will be heard. No message comes to me while I am waiting."

Shortly before her death, she held a glorified and garish séance on top of a Hollywood hotel. It was Halloween, 1936. The movie colony put on a great show—but the great showman was absent. Perhaps he thought once was enough.

There remains one more witness to be heard from. As to the significance of his message, I must admit that I am somewhat perplexed. However, he seems to add a properly fantastic ending to a fanatastic tale. The affair was reported in the *Los Angeles Times*.

One mist-shrouded dawn in 1938 Pat, Houdini's twenty-five-year-old pet parrot, picked the lock of his "escape proof" cage and flew into the Hollywood hills. There he scared residents with his weird cries.

It was said that during one of the attempts by Beatrice Houdini to communicate with her husband, Pat suddenly stopped his eternal monologue. After a long silence, he began to speak in a strange language. He had been taught only English. When he resumed English, he was less talkative than before.

Then he picked the special lock on his cage—in true tradition of the master—and flew into the hills singing, "Who's afraid of the big bad wolf."

Chapter 12

VANISHED CONTINENTS

MANY PERSONS are firmly convinced that there once existed vast continents peopled by races whose civilizations—at least spiritually—were more advanced than ours. The continents are supposed to have vanished beneath the ocean. Their end was sudden, perhaps even in "a day and a night." These are the sunken continents of the Sunday supplements. It may be that all this is true. Who can say?

To believers in such lost lands, this chapter will probably be disappointing. It contains data which I hope are thought provoking, but no conclusive proof. I have never found a single case which of itself proves the former existence of these legendary continents.

Those who have made the strongest cases for such lands have done so by piecing together vast amounts of suggestive, but individually inconclusive, data. This was the method of Bramwell, Spence, Braghine, Donnelly, etc.

It remains that no authentic and irrefutable written record of such a disaster has been found, nor has dredging the ocean floor brought up anything of a conclusive nature. This last is not surprising as by now sunken cities may be covered with thick blankets of silt and sludge. But if the sea has a secret, it keeps it well.

Many sincere believers in lost continents accept entirely different methods of proof—so-called "direct knowledge," information received through intuition and race memory, or from dead inhabitants of Lost Atlantis, or Mu, or Lemuria, speaking through the lips of mediums. Others base their beliefs on esoteric tradition, secret knowledge preserved through societies of initiates. Concerning these methods of ascertaining facts, I can only say that I do not consider myself competent to deal with them, and must therefore limit myself to methods with which I am more familiar.

It might be well to make one point clear. Modern science is convinced that continents once existed where now there is deep ocean. However, scientists are adamant on two points—

that these continents went down before man existed, and that they went down slowly. Nor has archeology ever accepted the existence of mighty and highly advanced civilizations before those of Egypt, Mesopotamia, and Crete.

However, it is not necessary to postulate a high civilization to give a recent continental catastrophe significance. Such an event would be epochal, both geologically and historically. More important, it has vital bearing on what may happen to the continents on which we are now living.

Modern lost continent speculation begins with a story in Plato's dialogues, *Timaeus* and *Critias,* to the effect that a great land known as Atlantis had sunk in a day and a night beyond the Pillars of Hercules, i.e., in the Atlantic ocean, and that a noble civilization had gone down with it.

In the eighteenth century several writers began where Plato left off, and produced extensive works seeking to prove the existence of Lost Atlantis. Since then numerous books on the subject have appeared.

Two more sunken continents have been proposed, Mu (or Moo or Pan), and Lemuria, both in the Pacific.

In selecting the material for this chapter I have tried to present evidence that catastrophic earth movements may have occurred suddenly and in very recent geological times. I have also included an interesting and little known archeological puzzle, and one documentary, although vague, sidelight on the Atlantis riddle.

As to the whole field of lost continent speculation, I know no better comment than that which James Bramwell makes in his *Lost Atlantis,* published in 1938:

". . . Atlantis has existed in the minds of civilized people and in their maps, too. The legend is like a colored thread running right through the existing fragment of man's pattern; it is a living tradition and will continue to be handed down until another deluge . . .

In the *Literary Digest,* January 31, 1925, there is a short article on mysteriously rising and sinking islands. This includes the following statement:

"The rising of a large area of the Atlantic bed, though the news of it passed almost unnoticed in the press, is one of the most vast and important of the changes in the earth's surface."

The article points out that in 1924 the Eastern Cable company sent a ship to repair a cable break which had occurred in the line between Cape Town and St. Helena. The exact spot of the break was eight hundred miles north of the Cape.

The ship duly found the break, and sent down grapnels to pick up the cable. It was found at a depth of approximately three-quarters of a mile. When the cable was laid in 1899, the ocean depth at that point had ben 2,700 fathoms, or just over three miles.

Far out in the Atlantic basin, the ocean floor had risen two miles in only twenty-five years.

OUT OF THE wind-tossed Atlantic emerged the dredge bucket which had been lowered from the Woods Hole Institute research ship. It was the summer of 1934 and the ship was working the ocean floor off Cape Cod in search of marine fossils.

This particular bucket brought up fossils, but along with them it brought up the shadow of Lost Atlantis. For the fossils were those of certain dry land creatures which indicated that the ocean floor had sunk *recently and suddenly.*

Startled by their discovery, the expedition continued dredging in deep water. They found evidence that a vast area had sunk as much as 8,000 feet within very recent geological times, very possibly within the memory of man.

Commenting on this matter in the *Bulletin of the Geological Society of America,* H. C. Stetson declared: ". . . such a rise and fall of sea bed in so short a time . . . *approaches the catastrophic.*"

ON All Saints' Day, 1755, one of the most disastrous earthquakes of all times struck Lisbon, Portugal. As the city disintegrated into rubble, thousands of inhabitants fled for safety to the new marble quay which flanked the harbor. Solid stone, *Cays de Prada* was built to last for eternity. Eternity is a long time.

At least ten thousand persons had assembled on the quay when a second earth shock ocurred. They were packed almost shoulder to shoulder, staring at the crumbling buildings of the city. A minute later *there was no quay*. It had vanished, dropping out of sight as if a giant hand had reached out of the sea and pulled it down.

Not only did the quay disappear in an instant, but the huge throng which had sought refuge upon it vanished utterly. Only churning water remained. A cosmic magician had completed one of the greatest disappearing acts of all time.

Not one body of the ten thousand engulfed ever floated to the surface. More astounding still, no piece of wood, no bits of clothing or ends of rope, no gear from the ships sucked down, was ever seen again. The earth opened and closed, and when it was done, the gigantic tomb was forever sealed.

WHEN AN entire archipelago—whose islands once stretched more than forty miles—vanishes off the face of the earth, it leaves behind it considerable problems. If an archipelago can sink, why not a continent? Thus reason the exponents of Lost Atlantis, Mu, and Lemuria.

In 1688 a Dutchman named Wafer published a book recounting his voyage in 1687 as first mate of the British ship, *The Bachelor's Delight,* commanded by John Davis. Wafer stated that at 27° 20′ south, they sighted an unknown island far off the west coast of South America, and hove to.

There they saw "to the westward . . . a range of high land which we took to be islands . . . This land seemed to reach in length about fourteen or fifteen leagues [something over forty miles.]" Later Captain Davis corroborated Wafer's account, and the archipelago was named *Davisland.*

During the next thirty-five years navigators sought in vain for Davisland, which appeared on every chart. No one ever found it. Davisland had vanished.

But it left behind problems, problems which indicate that Wafer and Davis may not have been mistaken. Two thousand miles west of the coast of Chile is brooding Easter Island, "the loneliest place on earth." Easter Island is strewn with gigantic forty-ton statues. Moreover, on this speck of land is found—baffling and indecipherable—the only written language of the South Pacific islands.

Professor J. MacMillan Brown in his *The Riddle of the Pacific,* could find no explanation for the culture of Easter Island *except by presuming a lost archipelago precisely where Davisland was reported.* He felt that Easter Island was the sacred cemetery for this chain of islands. He speculated:

". . . If only Davis had visited that long archipelago which stretched away to the northwest over the horizon, we should have *some inkling* of the culture and the power of the people who used Easter Island as a burial ground."

We might also know more about the whole puzzle of vanished lands. Unfortunately, Davis was in a hurry to reach home, and did not investigate.

IN 1939 five stone heads gave archeology a headache. The heads were of gigantic size, weighing approximately twenty-five tons each. They were discovered in a Mexican jungle near the western edge of the state of Tabasco.

It is hard enough to explain how the heads happened to be in that God forsaken jungle and what unknown people were able to produce such gigantic and artistic sculpture. But in addition to those problems is the matter of transportation.

The heads are of solid basalt. *There is no basalt nearer than one hundred miles from the spot where they were found.* Transporting twenty-five-ton heads through a hundred miles of jungle would be a problem for modern engineers, let alone primitive Indians.

Just one of a thousand similar small, mysterious discoveries. Perhaps each is purely local, and can be explained individually. Still, there remains the haunting feeling that the supposition of a highly civilized people, refugees from a sunken continent, would make the picture whole.

THE IRREPLACEABLE manuscripts which gave the key to the Mayan language were consigned to the flames on a sunny day in 1562. The destruction was ordered by the Spaniard, Diego de Landa. Those were the pages on which the ancient Mayans had inscribed the legends and history of their country.

More than three centuries later archeologists began to struggle with the riddle of Mayan culture, the puzzle of that mysterious race which filled the Yucatan jungles with pyramids and huge buildings rivaling the Egyptians. The scientists studied the pitifully few manuscripts which, either as originals or copies, escaped Landa's consuming fire. Probably the most important of these is the *Book of Chilam Balam* from Chumayel.

In 1930 the Brazilian scholar and philologist, A. M. Bolio, completed a translation of part of this manuscript.

Many passages in Bolio's translation suggest the hypothesis, supported by former Vice-President Charles G. Dawes, that the mystery of the Mayan culture originated in the death throes of Atlantis. The most significant portion of Bolio's translation is as follows:

"During the Eleventh Ahau Catoun it occurred . . . when the Earth began to waken. Nobody knew what was to come. And a fiery rain fell, and ashes fell, and rocks and trees fell down. And their Great Serpent was ravished from the heavens. And then, in one watery blow, came the waters . . . the sky fell down and the dry land sank. And in a moment the great annihilation was finished.

"And the Great Mother Seiba rose amidst recollections of the destruction of the earth."

Universal legend of a deluge, tales of vanished continents—they are part of the heritage of man. Who knows whether they are also part of his history?

Chapter 13

TALKING AND THINKING ANIMALS

THAT THERE have been animals that not only thought as men think, but communicated with men in man's language, seems incredible. In this chapter, perhaps more than anywhere else in this book, it is necessary to refuse the opiate of that traitorous word "impossible."

The proof of such strange doings on the part of animals is of first quality. The facts are attested by hundreds of ordinary men and women, and scores of eminent persons. Scientists, soldiers, writers, and philosophers have stated their unequivocal belief in the facts. The matter cannot be shrugged aside as unworthy of serious consideration.

The majority of the cases cluster around the work of a number of European experimenters. They are interlocking, each experimenter carrying on and improving the techniques of his predecessors. The final denouement of this work lies buried under the wreckage of two wars.

Similar experiments have been carried on in many parts of the world. One such case included in this chapter is that of Lady. This horse was particularly known as a telepathic animal, but her case follows the same general pattern as the others.

There are many other reliable cases besides those I have presented, but they tend to become repetitious.

The explanations of fraud, or conscious (or subconscious) signaling by the trainer are scarcely worth mentioning. They have been discredited time after time. In most tests conditions were such as to rule them out entirely.

Several other explanations have been advanced:

1. That certain animals, having proper heredity, and being carefully trained by the methods of successful experimenters, can develop minds and thinking processes comparable to children. The key to the whole puzzle, according to this school of thought, is to teach the animals language so that they may think in words, as men do.

2. That the answer lies in telepathy between the animals and living human beings.

3. That the brains and bodies of the animals are controlled or "possessed" by disincarnate intelligences of human quality. (For a case of alleged human possession, see that of Lurancy Vennum in "Riffraff and Rabble.")

4. That, as most of the animals were gifted in mathematics, the problems should be considered as part of

the mystery of child mathematical geniuses. This is scarcely an explanation at all, but merely a method of avoiding the question. It is explaining the incredible by the miraculous.

At least these cases suggest that, although man is temporarily master of the earth, he should not be too glib in expounding certainties about the minds of creatures that are not of his species.

MUCH OF modern psychology's present dilemma began with a horse.

She was a three-year-old black and white mare named Lady. Her owner, Mrs. C. D. Fonda of Richmond, Virginia, claimed that the horse could be controlled by telepathy. In 1927 Dr. J. B. Rhine investigated the case. Because of his results, he began his now famous work in telepathy at Duke University.

Several experiments with Lady were conducted between December 3, 1927, and January 15, 1928. Under the control of Dr. Rhine and great psychologist Dr. William McDougall, Lady followed directions given *mentally* by any member of the group. She picked out numbers and letters by pointing with her nose to child's alphabetical blocks which were placed on a small table before her.

The test conditions were steadily tightened until at last Lady's mistress was entirely absent from the room, and a screen was placed between the horse and the person seeking to give telepathic directions. Still she was successful.

She also carried on conversations, answering verbal questions. The following are examples:

Question: "Where can I borrow money?"
Lady's answer: "Bank."
Question: "Which bank?"
Lady's answer: "Commerce."
"Question: "What is this gentleman's name?"
Lady's answer: "Rhine."

In addition, she spelled words and solved mathematical problems, including cubed roots. A report of the investigation was published in *The Journal of Abnormal and Social Psychology*, 1928-9.

Dr. Rhine could find no normal explanation. He considered

that at least part of the phenomena were telepathic. And, he reasoned, if telepathy were possible between man and animal, surely it would be possible between man and man.

So it was the nose of a black and white horse and a set of child's alphabetical blocks that suggested the experiments which have left the old, simple, crudely materialistic psychology a mocking ruin.

THE HORSES of Elberfeld, those unbelievable equines, have long since gone from earthly meadows, pursued by psychologists claiming that what they did was impossible.

But the facts remain that the horses rapped out with their hoofs intelligent answers to simple questions and complex mathematical problems, that one horse was blind and therefore could not be influenced by visual signals, that they were tested by remote control with no one in the same room or even the same part of the stables.

The horses were kept at Elberfeld in Germany. They were trained by Karl Krall, a man who profoundly believed that animal intelligence varies from ours only because of a difference in symbols.

The horses rapped with their front hoofs on a special board. They were taught by means of a blackboard. For spelling, a simplified alphabet was used, each letter or diphthong being represented by a number between eleven and sixty-six. They spelled phonetically.

Investigated early in this century by eminent European scientists, the horses answered questions, spelled the investigators' names, and solved mathematical problems. One problem, (cube root of 5832), was written on the blackboard and a horse, Muhamed, was asked to solve it.

This particular problem was suggested and written by one of the scientists, and to eliminate telepathy, none of those present worked out the answer. In a matter of seconds Muhamed gave the answer, 18.

If the witnesses were deluded, the delusion seems to have been on a grand scale. A few of the men who testified to the reality of the facts were: Dr. Edinger, outstanding neurologist of Frankfort; Dr. Paul Sarasin of Bâle; Professor A. Beredka of the Pasteur Institute, Paris; Professor E. Claparède of the University of Geneva; Dr. R. Assagioli of Florence; Dr. Hartkopf of Köln; Dr. Freudenburg of Brussels.

JUST BEFORE World War I, Rolf, talking dog trained by Frau Dr. Moekel, was tested in the hall of the Casino at Mannheim, Germany. The date was May 11, 1914. Chief of the examining scientists was Professor H. E. Ziegler of Stuttgart.

By tapping with his paw, the dog solved mathematical problems called out by the audience. Then he began to answer questions, using a code to indicate letters of the alphabet. After he had given several correct answers, Professor Ziegler conducted the final test.

The professor had brought with him a box inside which was a papier maché maybug. Inside the maybug was a dog biscuit. To prevent any possibility of signaling, Frau Dr. Moekel left the hall. Then the box was opened before Rolf. He smelled the maybug, but did not attempt to open it

Frau Dr. Moekel then returned and asked the dog what it found in the box.

"Maybug," Rolf replied instantly, "inside that something to eat." Then as an afterthought: "Didn't eat it."

Dr. Ziegler stated that he believed the dog thought and expressed himself exactly as men do—but the good doctor was wrong. For although Rolf's trainer attempted for years to teach him the meaning of the word "war," the dog died without understanding it.

LOLA, an airedale, was born at Mannheim, Germany, on January 27, 1914. She was the daughter of Rolf (see last case). The details of her career are given in the work, *Lola*, by Henny Kindermann. The book was originally in German, but there is an excellent English edition, translation by Agnes Blake.

Henny Kindermann was Lola's trainer. After two years of patient work, she claimed the following results. The dog—using the paw tapping code—could add, divide, subtract, and multiply. She could answer intelligently any simple question, whether put by her mistress or a stranger.

She knew the days of the week, the months of the year. She understood and could use appropriately such abstract terms as "love," "hate," "fear," "hope," etc.

Lola was investigated by psychologist Dr. William MacKenzie of Genoa, Professor Kraemer of Hohenheim, and Professor H. E. Ziegler. Each certified the facts as given above.

IN 1937 death came to Kurwenal. He was a dachshund. He was also the last and the greatest of the dogs trained by German noblewoman, Mathilde, Baroness von Freytag-Loringhoven.

The Baroness refined previous techniques, and taught Kurwenal to speak in a *bark alphabet* in which each letter was assigned a certain number of barks.

The whole case was reviewed in *The American Kennel Gazette* for March 1, 1938.

Once Professor Dr. Siegmund-Schultze of Berlin came to Weimar to investigate the dog, bringing with him a packet of biscuits. He showed Kurwenal the packet and asked the trade name.

"Knapsack," was the barked reply. It was correct. As an afterthought, Kurwenal added, "A knapsack is a bag carried on the back."

Another scientist asked him which he preferred—cheese or biscuits.

"Cheese," he barked, "because it tastes better."

After Professor Plate of Jena had spent some time testing him, Kurwenal barked: "If only he would stop trying to trick me."

He talked daily with those around him, his mind appearing to be that of a ten-year-old child.

General von Hoff of Stuttgart wrote a pamphlet on the dog, attesting—"on his honor as a general"—the truth of the animal's strange powers.

The dog carried on long spontaneous conversations when *alone* with the investigators, often when his mistress was miles away. He could calculate faster than most of the scientists.

Once Kurwenal was asked: "What do you think of death?" He barked in reply: "I am not afraid."

It would appear that either many eminent men inexplicably became so befuddled that they could not intelligently investigate one small dog—or else a mind of human status, in the body of a dachshund, died in 1937.

Chapter 14

MISPLACED IN TIME

IN THEIR HEARTS men have always felt that the veil of the future occasionally wore thin, so that coming events were more than shadows. Why men should persistently believe this is in itself something of a mystery.

This belief has been meat and bread to a thousand generations of soothsayers. Usually, the only equipment necessary was a robe, a turban, and a monstrous aversion to physical labor. Very occasionally there may have been far more—an ability to tinker with the thing we call Time.

The conception of a single absolute time, eternally winding off the spool of the future and on to the spool of the past, has been subjected during this century to a number of assaults. Its impregnability is no longer quite so awesome.

Albert Einstein, he who suggested to President Roosevelt that an atomic bomb might conceivably be practical, reduced time to the status of a dimension. Physicists have been muttering that time may not be absolute, and that there may be several varieties of it.

In the meantime another strange idea has risen wraith-like from the pit of the infinite. The man responsible for this particular bit of magic is J. W. Dunne, a British military engineer. He suggested, and backed his suggestion with an array of facts, that all men occasionally dream of events before they occur. His method of organizing proof may be new, but the basic conception of precognitive dreams is at least as old as the race.

Later, Dunne enlarged his ideas into a philosophy. Being an engineer, he used diagrams to explain time dimensions. Some people find his philosophy easily understandable; to others it is utterly incomprehensible. I have included a brief discussion of Dunne's work.

This chapter deals with many other tales besides those from the world of dreams. A number of stories are given which indicate that people have sometimes experienced time in a different way than it is calculated by a wrist watch. Sometimes this was in the world of dreams, sometimes it occurred in the more orderly world of wide-awake. I have included two odd little tales, those concerning Wolfe and Swift.

As to professional prophets, I have been very exclusive in my selection, including only Nostradamus. He stands head and shoulders above the other members of his rowdy profession. Almost without exception, prophets are vague, devoid of specific details, predicting such absolute certainties as "wars and rumors of wars." Most of them are—or should be—without honor in any country.

I have included one case of backwards misplacement in time. This is the story of the two women at Versailles. The supernormality of the Versailles incident has been questioned, and with considerable effect, by J. R. Sturge-Whiting. I have appended to the story a brief outline of this debate.

I certainly do not suggest that the tales in this chapter prove that the future is irrevocably fixed, irrespective of human struggle. Determinism is, and always will be, an empty concept. It is one of those sterile ideas which well from the egotism of *Ich und Gott.*

But there are indications that our present idea of time needs some revision, just as the older physics, with its immutable ninety-two elements, needed enlargement. If these stories suggest anything, it is that, so far as time goes, we "see through a glass darkly." In any case, they are queer tales.

SEVERAL TIMES J. W. Dunne felt that he had experienced a certain occurrence before. This is common to all men. Dunne thought the key to the mystery was in dreams that included future events. He therefore kept a careful record of his dreams, with startling results.

Later, he collected and correlated the dreams of a large number of persons, and believed that he had established the phenomenon of dreamland glimpses into the future. He presented his case in *An Experiment with Time,* 1927. The following dream is an example of Dunne's personal excursions into tomorrow.

While camped with the Mounted Infantry in the Orange Free State, South Africa, during the spring of 1902, Dunne dreamed that he was on an island. He suddenly realized that the island was about to explode. Desperately he tried to induce the French authorities to evacuate the populace, stating that unless they did, forty thousand persons would be killed. His warning went unheeded and the island duly exploded.

Some days after the dream Dunne received a newspaper describing the explosion of Mt. Pelee on the French island of Martinique. The disaster had occurred *after* Dunne's dream.

Although repeatedly warned, the French authorities had refused to evacuate the populace. As a result, forty thousand persons died. The volcano had cracked in exactly the way Dunne had observed in his dream.

The rest of Dunne's evidence is similar. Some of his most significant dreams, from the standpoint of proving knowledge of future events, are extremely dull. Dull dreams are the burden of most men. However, there are some highly dramatic nocturnal wanderings. Such are the next two stories.

OF ALL THE TALES brought back from the shadow world of sleep, few are stranger or better authenticated than that of Frederick Lane.

On Thursday night, December 16, 1897, William Terriss, British actor, was to appear in a mediocre melodrama, "Secret Service," at the Adelphi Theater, London. Terriss' understudy was a man named Frederick Lane.

On the afternoon of the sixteenth, Lane appeared at rehearsal, and buttonholing everyone in sight, described a dream which had come to him the night before. He had dreamed that Terriss, surrounded by actors and stage hands, was lying in a state of semi-consciousness on the stairs leading to the dressing rooms. His chest was bare, and he was apparently injured.

Later, Miss Alice Johnson, associate of the Newnham College, Cambridge, collected affidavits from three persons to whom Lane had told his dream on Thursday afternoon. The persons were actress Frances Olive Haygate, and actors H. Carter Bligh, and S. Creagh Henry. All the affidavits agreed as to the details of the dream.

Mr. Terriss played a very unexpected role at the Adelphi Theater that night of December 16, and the affair became a front page sensation in the London newspapers. The *London Times* for December 17 included the dream incident in its story of *how Terriss had been murdered by a madman who stabbed him as he entered the theater.*

In describing the scene of Terriss' death, the *Times* stated that he was carried inside the theater and placed *on the foot of the dressing room stairs. There, semi-conscious, his chest bared and members of the company around him,* he died.

DURING THE NIGHT of June 27-28, 1914, Monsigneur Joseph de Lanyi, Bishop of Grosswarden, was afflicted with a most disturbing dream. In this he saw on his study table a black-edged letter bearing the arms of a certain Archduke whom the Bishop had once instructed in the Hungarian language.

Bishop de Lanyi opened the letter, read its contents, and awoke in terror. He noted down the time, which was 4:30 A.M., and the contents of the dream letter. When the Bishop's servant came to wake him at six o'clock, he found de Lanyi, much agitated, telling his rosary.

The churchman then summoned his mother and his host, and read to them the contents of his dream letter, as given in his notes. It read as follows:

"Your Eminence,
 Dear Mr. Lanyi
 My wife and I have been victims of a political crime at Sarajevo. We commend ourselves to your prayers.
                              Sarajevo. June 28, 1914."

It was signed by Franz Ferdinand, Archduke of Austria,

who ten hours later died at Sarajevo, victim of an assassin's bullet—the first bullet of World War I.

ONE OF THE world's classic ghost stories was told by famous British diplomat Lord Dufferin. It is also a story that does violence to Time.

While he was staying at a friend's country house in Ireland, Lord Dufferin awakened one night in a state of meaningless dread. To quiet his nerves, he arose and stood by the window.

In the bright moonlight outside a man walked slowly across the lawn. On his back he carried a large box. As he passed the window, he turned and looked at Dufferin.

The man's face was of an indescribable ugliness. Just as the man was passing out of sight, Dufferin realized the object he was carrying was a coffin.

The next day Dufferin made a number of inquiries as to the man's identity, but could learn nothing.

Years later, when Dufferin was ambassador to Paris, he was about to enter an elevator on his way to an important diplomatic gathering when he glanced at the elevator operator. *It was the man he had seen years before carrying the coffin through the moonlit Irish woods.*

Instinctively Dufferin stepped back. The cage started upwards. When it had ascended three floors, the cable broke and the elevator crashed to the basement. A number of prominent persons were killed, others injured.

Investigation revealed that the elevator operator, who was killed in the accident, had been hired for that day only. His identity still remains a mystery.

(There are two versions of this story, one gives Lord Dufferin's experience in Ireland as a dream rather than a waking vision. Obviously, this discrepancy has no bearing on the prophetic aspects of the story.)

NOSTRADAMUS, French physician and prophet, is one of the few soothsayers ever to give specific names and details of occurrences in the future. Not all of his prophecies have come to pass, but the fulfillment of a few has been striking. In addition to prophesying, he was credited, as a physician, with devising the only successful remedy for victims of the Black Plague.

In his first "Prophetic Centuries," a series of predictions cast in the form of quatrains and published in 1555, he prophesied that King Henry II of France "would be blinded in a golden cage." In 1559 Henry was blinded by a dueling lance which smashed through the visor of his golden helmet.

Also in the first edition of the "Centuries," Nostradamus said: "The Lily of the Dauphin will come to Nancy, and carry aid in Flanders to an Elector of the Empire. The great Montmorency will be placed in a new prison, and away from the usual place, he will be delivered to Clerepeyne."

Certainly this jumble of words made no sense in 1555. But more than three-quarters of a century later, the troops of Louis XIII, who held the title of the Dauphin, entered Nancy, and later invaded Flanders to aid the Elector of Trier. "The Great" Montmorency was incarcerated in the newly completed prison of Toulouse, and later beheaded, away from the usual place for executions, by a soldier named Clerepeyne.

Of the French Revolution, then over two hundred years in the future, Nostradamus predicted that the Tuileries would be stormed by five hundred, that the King would be crowned with a cockade, that men named Narbon and Sauce would be involved.

When the Tuileries were invaded, June 20, 1792, the red cockade of the Jacobins was placed on the head of Louis XVI. Count Narbonne was war minister under Louis. Sauce was the name of the small tradesman who recognized the King on his attempted flight from France.

Another of Nostradamus' prophecies contains what might well be a reference to Napoleon:

"Of the name that a French King never was,
There was never a lightning so much feared,
Italy shall tremble; Spain and the English;
He shall be much taken by women strangers."

Various attempts to link some of Nostradamus' prophecies with recent events, particularly those of World War II, have not been too successful. Perhaps these prophecies were not meant for our time, or possibly as the seer looked farther into the future his vision became clouded.

WHERE Jonathan Swift got the astronomy he included in his *Gulliver's Travels* is a problem.

In the original edition of the book, published in 1726,
Swift had Gulliver visit the mythical island of Laputa, whose
astronomers were famed for their skill. The star gazers of
this land had discovered that Mars had two moons, one of
which traveled twice as fast as the other.

In 1726 the astronomers of the real world maintained that
Mars was moonless. One hundred and fifty years later, in
1877, the Naval Observatory at Washington, D.C., discovered that Mars had two moons, *one of which traveled
twice as fast as the other.*

THE FOLLOWING are the facts of the connection between American writer Thomas Wolfe and "K 19." Pre-
monition or coincidence—take your choice.

Shortly after the publication of his work, *Look Homeward
Angel,* Wolfe sent his publishers another book which centered
around a pullman car numbered "K 19." In fact, "K 19" was
to be the title of the work. The manuscript was not published, but Wolfe later incorporated part of it in *Of Time
and the River.*

Still, he could not escape the fascination of "K 19." In his
last work, *You Can't Go Home Again,* pullman "K 19" appeared.

Wolfe died on September 15, 1938. His friend and editor,
Edward C. Aswell—who recounts the incident in *The Hills
Beyond,* 1941—was present when the author's body was
placed on the train to be taken to his home in Asheville,
North Carolina. Wolfe's family also boarded the train.

As the train pulled away, Aswell noted the number "K 19"
on the pullman in which the writer's family rode.

IN THE SUMMER of 1939, a few weeks before Chamber-
lain's umbrella finally folded, Mrs. Axel Wenner-Grens, wife
of the Swedish industrialist, chanced to precede her husband
up the stairs of their home. It was just after midnight and
the house was heavy with shadow.

Suddenly the figure of a water-drenched man appeared at the head of the stairs. He held out the body of a child. Across the child's forehead was a great, bleeding gash. Mrs. Wenner-Grens screamed, and the figure vanished.

Herr Wenner-Grens listened with unbelief to his wife's story. He put the whole thing down to strained nerves, and suggested a cruise on their yacht, the *Southern Cross*.

When in answer to frantic distress signals on the night of September 3, 1939, the *Southern Cross* reached the spot where the torpedoed *Athenia* had sunk, Mrs. Wenner-Grens assisted in the rescue of survivors.

The first person to reach the deck of the *Southern Cross* was a drenched man. He held out the body of a dying child across whose forehead was a deep bleeding gash. Those are the facts, as Wenner-Grens later related them to a newspaper man in Victoria, British Columbia.

BEFORE TWO women was part of the garden of Versailles as it existed in 1789—but the date was August 10, 1901. When the women had stepped into that area of the quiet garden they had stepped backward in time. At least that was what they said.

The women were Charlotte E. A. Moberley and Eleanor Jourdain. Both occupied highly important educational posts. They had gone to Versailles as sightseers. As they walked along the twisting paths the scenery became unreal, stage-like. They felt as if they had entered a strange "circle of influence," an eerie world of shadows and fear.

The garden around them was not the showplace of 1901, it was the garden of Marie Antoinette. This was the garden in which one of the great dramas of all time was building towards its last scene, when a piece of falling steel would meet a queen's white neck.

For some time the two women wandered through this scene which was correctly placed in space, *but misplaced in time*. Figures moved in the garden, figures out of the past. They saw before them buildings as they existed in those last days when the tolerance of the French masses was fast running out. They observed people who belonged to that long dead time.

109

Then they walked on, and suddenly entered the normal world, whose time agreed with the calendar. Both women had observed the same scene; the notes which they made were meticulously accurate. In every detail they seemed to have walked backward in time.

For ten years the women searched through documents, trying to identify each detail of the vision. Each bit of corroborating evidence was carefully deposited in the Bodleian Library at Oxford. Everything was checked, location of trees and shrubbery, dress of the court, hundreds of minute details. After a decade they believed they had succeeded in completely verifying the vision.

The Versailles "ghost story," published in 1911 under title *An Adventure,* created a considerable furore, but no organized attack was thrown against it for many years, possibly because of the high standing of the two witnesses.

In 1938 an Englishman, J. R. Sturge-Whiting, published his *The Mystery of Versailles,* which he declared was "a complete solution" to the enigma. By then both Miss Moberley and Miss Jourdain were dead.

Sturge-Whiting had done a large amount of research, and believed he had proved that the mystery was a brew concocted out of bad observation, mood, faulty memory, and an incurable desire for romance. He makes out a good case, a case which seems to be just short of adequate.

In the later edition of *An Adventure,* Miss Edith Olivier says, relative to Sturge-Whiting's solution of the mystery: ". . . the impression given is that the story itself, with its crowd of substantiating evidence, is today as alive and vivid as it ever was; the criticisms, on the other hand, are singularly dead and out of date."

It may be that the truth lies somewhere between the two points of view. Perhaps the women tried to make too perfect a case out of what was only an imperfect glimpse—but a glimpse nevertheless.

IRENE KUHN tells this story in her *Assigned to Adventure,* 1938:

She was walking, happy and whistling, down Michigan Boulevard, Chicago, when the scene before her suddenly faded. For an instant she saw before her a grass-covered hill across which spring sunlight spread feebly. On the hill were three peculiarly shaped trees.

There was a small iron fence and in the background smokestacks of a factory. A black limousine drove up, and a white faced woman alighted. She was assisted to a spot where a small hole had been dug in the grass. A tiny box lay in the hole.

And then suddenly she saw only Michigan Boulevard and the stained snow that a screaming blizzard had brought the night before.

The following May, Irene Kuhn was driven in a black limousine to a cemetery she had never seen, where the ashes of her husband, who had died suddenly in China a month before, were returned to the earth.

Before her was the spring sunlight, the rusty iron fence, the grassy hill, the three peculiar trees, the factory in the background, and the small box in the little hole—just as it had been in the momentary vision on snow-banked Michigan Boulevard.

Chapter 15

VALLEY OF THE SHADOW

". . . There is only a moment of shadow between your life and mine."

So speaks Death in the play *Death Takes a Holiday*. To Death—and certain human beings who claim to understand all things—the matter may be that simple. To most of us it remains somewhat obscure.

Hosts of tales have been told about the "moment of shadow," and there have been a number of interesting scientific investigations concerning it. However, experiments conducted on human beings at the moment of death are fragmentary. But those which have been made were undertaken in the spirit of science and by men trained in that art. Whether scientific techniques are helpful in this field is uncertain—mainly because they have been so seldom applied.

As to whether human personalities survive bodily death, most persons make up their minds, one way or the other, on the basis of faith—either in revealed religion or established materialism. Faith is a very important, and often noble, part of life.

A few people have conducted rather elaborate investigations of the problem. I have presented one of those, that of Dr. Thomas.

Countless stories have been recounted about souls who took time off from heavenly pursuits to briefly revisit the world of the living. It is said that this has sometimes been done to fulfill a compact. I have included two such stories, and one tale about a British aviator who seemed still irked over faulty aircraft construction.

The stories presented in this chapter are factually valid; beyond this I do not take up the sword and shield of argument.

NEWSPAPERS SAID that Dr. Duncan MacDougall had "weighed the soul." Dr. MacDougall replied that he had merely conducted an interesting experiment. There was an uproar, but it soon subsided. To the best of my knowledge and belief, Dr. MacDougall's experiments have never been repeated.

Dr. MacDougall was a physician on the staff of the Massachusetts General Hospital. He conducted his experiments in 1906, and published a complete report in the *Journal* of the American Society for Psychical Research, May, 1907. His technique was as follows:

A light framework was built on a delicately balanced scales. This framework held a bed on which the patient, in a dying condition, was placed. The scales were sensitive to within one-tenth of an ounce.

All of the subjects gave their consent to the experiment weeks before their deaths. Dr. MacDougall chose patients suffering from diseases which terminated in profound exhaustion, death occurring with little or no muscular movement. This prevented agitation of the scales.

As the entire bed was weighed along with the patient, any matter escaping from the patient's body would in no way affect the results. Even the weight of the air exhausted from the patient's lungs was taken into consideration, and was found too slight to have any bearing on the experiment.

As will be seen from the following typical case, evaporation, progressing at a steady rate, was also taken into account:

". . . subject was a man dying of tuberculosis. The patient was under observation for three hours and forty minutes before death. . . He lost weight slowly at the rate of one ounce per hour, due to evaporation of moisture in respiration and evaporation of sweat.

"During all three hours and forty minutes I kept the beam end [of the scales] slightly above balance near the upper limiting bar in order to make the test more decisive if it should come.

"At the end of three hours and forty minutes he expired, and suddenly, coincident with death, the beam end dropped with an *audible stroke*, hitting against the lower limiting bar and remaining there with no rebound. The loss was ascertained to be three-fourths of an ounce."

Dr. MacDougall experimented with six patients, and in every case found a distinct sudden drop of weight at the instant of death. In some of the cases a second sudden loss occurred.

Two of the cases Dr. MacDougall ruled out as inconclusive, one because interference by persons opposed to his work made accurate observations impossible, and the other because the patient died so soon after having been placed on the bed that the scales were not in perfect adjustment. In the remaining four cases conditions for accurate observations were perfect.

Dr. MacDougall was assisted in his experiments by several of his medical colleagues. It was certainly a curious investigation.

PSYCHICAL RESEARCHER Dr. Hereward Carrington once learned that a girl whom he knew was dying in Greenwich Village. He decided to observe the girl's body at the moment of death through one of the dicyanin screens devised by Dr. Kilner for the purpose of making visible the human aura or semi-material double (see discussion of Dr. Kilner's work in "Forgotten Experiments").

A friend of Dr. Carrington's also participated in the experiment. Both were observing the girl's body through Kilner's filters as death occured. They believed they saw a smoke-like, tenuous mist rise from the body. As Carrington described the phenomena:

"We both saw it. At first it seemed stationary, clinging to the outline of the body. Then it seemed to gather life and movement, shifting slightly away. A more clearly defined bodily shape appeared, as though floating in space directly above the body. For a few moments this was visible to us. Then it moved off into the deeper shadows of the far corner of the room and was lost to sight."

Dr. Carrington recounts another personal experience which, although not connected with death watch experimentation, at least bears obliquely on the subject. It is particularly interesting in view of Dr. Carrington's sceptical attitude in such matters.

One day he was seated at his desk when he had an irresistible urge to phone a certain young woman. He did so and was informed that she had died the day before. Immediately there began a series of strange occurrences in Dr. Carrington's apartment.

First there were a number of loud knocks which could not be traced to any normal cause. Then Dr. Carrington, together with several persons who visited him, had an overwhelming feeling that some one was standing in one corner of a certain room.

Next the knocker on the apartment door was banged loudly several times. Dr. Carrington was standing just inside the door, and instantly jerked it open. The hall outside was empty.

Lastly a key of the piano was struck several times. There was no one in the room. No pet animals were in the apartment. There seemed no normal explanation for the key's being struck.

Carrington concluded:

"What *appeared* to be happening was that some invisible

entity had endeavored to attract my attention, and when it had finally succeeded in doing so . . . it was 'satisfied' and took its departure!"

SEEMINGLY OF the same ilk as Dr. Carrington's vigil over the dying girl in Greenwich Village, is a case recounted by Dr. James H. Hyslop, then professor of logic and ethics at Columbia University.

One of those little groups which are as old as life had formed around the bed of Louisa M. Alcott's sister. The group was composed of Louisa M. Alcott, her mother, and the family doctor. They were waiting, as such groups do, for the physiological change which we call death.

It came. The mechanism ceased to function; the doctor made the prescribed examination.

For a moment longer the group remained at the bedside. As they watched, a strange thing happened. A thin faintly glowing mist arose from the body, swiftly coalesced, and floated away.

Miss Alcott stated: "Mother's eyes followed mine and when I said, 'What did you see?' she described the same light mist."

The doctor said that he too had seen the dimly luminescent mist. He could offer no explanation, saying only that there was a world-old belief that something left the body at the moment of death.

PHOTOGRAPHING OF a tenuous vapor-like thing detaching itself from the body at the moment of death was claimed by Dr. Hippolyte Baraduc, French physician and neurologist. A few scattered attempts to duplicate Dr. Baraduc's results have not been successful. I give the facts as Dr. Baraduc recorded them.

He conducted his first experiment in April, 1907, using as the subject his son, André Joseph Baraduc, photographs being taken at death and at intervals of three hours thereafter.

The results achieved were interesting enough to cause Dr. Baraduc to repeat his experiments six months later when his wife died. This time exposures were made at the moment of death and every fifteen minutes thereafter for a period of three hours.

When developed, the plates showed three distinct balls of mist rising from the dead woman's body. These balls slowly coalesced until they formed a single globe. This remained for some time attached to the body by a single luminous cord. At last this cord broke and the globe floated away.

SELDOM HAS the valley of shadow been invaded by as systematic a researcher as Dr. John F. Thomas, psychologist at Duke University. Dr. Thomas thought that even such mundane things as graphs, charts, and organization might be helpful in untangling the puzzle of the ages.

After the death of his wife, Dr. Thomas conducted an elaborate experiment to discover whether a personality which —through certain unimpeachable psychics—represented itself as Mrs. Thomas, could give him supernormal information. In the end, the investigation became the subject of his doctorate at Duke.

As an extra precaution against fraud, or telepathy from his own mind, Thomas arranged for the majority of sittings with psychics to be conducted in his absence. In fact, they were held in England while he was in America, the statements of the psychics being taken down by a stenographer. The stenographer, incidentally, knew nothing of Thomas's personal life.

For six years the investigation went on. All of the points discussed by the personality claiming to be Mrs. Thomas were graphed and charted. They were classified under such headings as *correct, incorrect, inconclusive, unverifiable.*

Thousands of different items were considered. The pages of Dr. Thomas's work, *Beyond Normal Cognition,* contain lengthy lists of specific statements dealing not only with the life which Dr. and Mrs. Thomas lived together, but also with Thomas' life after his wife's death.

There are endless references—to a ball game they attended, to the color and design of a rug they once owned, to occurrences in Mrs. Thomas's early life of which Dr. Thomas himself had never heard, to the names and personalities of men and women they had met, to a book—even to the exact page—which Thomas in America had been reading the day before the sitting in England between the psychic and the stenographer.

The analysis of the case ends with a summing up of the evidence and a calculation of the percentage of correct points given at each sitting with the different psychics. *The number of correct statements for all the sittings is better than seventy percent.*

ENTOMBED IN the pages of the *Encyclopaedia Britannica* is the story of Frederic Myers, and his "cross-correspondence."

Myers was prominent in England as a poet, essayist, and scholar. After becoming interested in psychical research, he took up biology and psychology, and later became a first-flight psychologist in his own right.

After years of investigating supernormal phenomena, he concluded that life after death had ben proved. The only weak link he could find in his theory was the possibility that all supernormal information actually originated in telepathy from living persons.

Myers died in 1901. At the time of his death he was in a state of great physical agony and great mental calm. He said that his researches had taken from him all fear of death, which he had decided was but a minor incident of conscious existence. He regretted, however, that he never found a way to make his case for imortality foolproof by ruling out the chance of telepathy from living persons.

Shortly after his death, a personality which claimed to be Myers made its appearance in the automatic writing produced by several non-professional psychics.

(Automatic writing is a process in which the alleged psychic writes a script without consciously knowing what is written. No one claims that the writing is done by supernormal means. The importance of the script lies in any supernormal information which it may contain.)

The messages which were received from what purported to be the personality of Myers were in a style characteristic of the dead psychologist, and they contained many bits of information *which would not be known to the psychics, but would have been known by Myers.*

Soon after the messages began, a new development was noticed. Half a dozen psychics would find meaningless sentences in their scripts. The sentences would be in the style of Myers; but they would be entirely disconnected.

At last it was discovered that *if the sentences were put in a certain order, they made a coherent whole.* Therefore, not only did the content appear supernormal, but the pattern of the complete messages seemed dictated by some personality outside of the psychics, a personality which sent disconnected parts of each message to different psychics.

This complicated scheme would practically rule out telepathy from living persons and so supply the missing link in Myers' chain of evidence for survival, the link he could not forge while alive.

If Myers did do this thing—if he was so determined to prove a point that he went on hammering at it even after death, he should be given credit for considerable perseverance.

THE NAME OF Lord Henry Peter Brougham (1778-1868) is deeply embedded in modern English history. He was once described in the words: "a vigor and variety of intellect almost unparalleled . . . one of the most extraordinary and illustrious men of his age . . ." So much for the man on whose word the following story rests.

After Lord Brougham's death, it was found that he had kept a lifetime diary. In this he mentioned a certain friend with whom he had been particularly intimate while at the University of Edinburgh. Later this friend left the university and took a post in the Indian civil service. Soon afterwards Lord Brougham graduated from the university, and after a few years, engrossed in his career, had forgotten the existence of his school days' friend.

In December, 1799, Lord Brougham, then traveling in Sweden, made the following entry in his diary: "Having set out for Gothenburg . . . about one in the morning we arrived at a decent inn and stopped for the night . . . I was glad to take advantage of a hot bath before I turned in.

And here a most remarkable thing happend to me . . .

". . . while lying in my bath, I turned my head round, looking towards the chair on which I had deposited my clothes. On the chair sat 'G' [Brougham's friend at the university] looking calmly at me. At once, the apparition or whatever it was disappeared."

(The fact that Lord Brougham cloaked his friend in anonymity is unfortunate. That era was particularly afflicted with this weakness. However, Lord Brougham's standing and the fact that the incident appears in his diary seems sufficient authentication.)

This particular diary entry was dated December 19. Later Lord Brougham had added, "Soon after my return to Edinburgh, there arrived a letter from India, announcing the death of my friend, and stating that he died on the 19th of December!"

In that same December 19th entry of Brougham's diary there is one other sentence that is worthy of consideration. It reads:

"When we were at the university, my friend and I committed the folly of drawing up an agreement, written in our blood, to the effect that whichever of us died first would appear to the other."

DR. VINCENZO CALTAGIRONE, agnostic physician of Palermo, Italy, sat chatting with his friend and patient, Benjamin Sirchia, Italian statesman. It was May of 1910, and the talk turned to strange tales. Sirchia suggested lightly that he might return after death. Dr. Caltagirone replied:

"Then you'll come and manifest yourself by breaking something in this room—for example, the gas fixture above the table. (We were at that moment in my dining room.)"

Sirchia agreed. A few days later he left for another part of the country, where he died unexpectedly late the following November. Dr. Caltagirone did not know of his death. He had long since forgotten the half-joking conversation about the death pact.

Two days after Sirchia's death *something* started banging on a little glass bell which hung at the top of the dining room gas fixture. Dr. Caltagirone and his sister investigated.

119

They climbed on the table. They could find no explanation.

For six days something continued off and on to bang on the glass bell. Then at last the bell split. The pieces were *deposited* on the table under the fixture. The witnesses swore that the pieces could not have fallen under the fixture, as the fixture itself was in the way. They could only have been *laid* under the lamp.

The story is given in great detail, and first hand. Camille Flammarion published Dr. Caltagirone's account in his *Death and Its Mystery—After Death.*

IN THE fog-dripping dawn of Sunday, October 5, 1930, the British dirigible R-101 crashed near Beauvais, France. In one flame-seared instant sudden death came to her commander, Flight Lieutenant H. C. Irwin, along with forty-five of her crew.

On Thursday, October 2, 1930, Harry Price had arranged with psychic Mrs. Eileen Garrett to work with him in his laboratory on October 7. The psychic arrived as scheduled.

Mrs. Garrett is a cultured Irish woman, and a non-professional psychic. She is particularly known for her work with Dr. J. B. Rhine at Duke University. At present she publishes and edits the American magazine *Tomorrow.* This periodical carries a wide variety of material of general interest and only occasionally features an article on the supernormal.

Harry Price, who has been mentioned earlier, is a scientist and psychical researcher of the highest standing.

On that October 7 in Price's laboratory, Mrs. Garrett went into a trance, and almost immediately a very irate aviator began to speak through her lips. He claimed he was Flight Lieutenant Irwin, commander of the R-101.

Lieutenant Irwin discussed the crash, declared: "Useful lift too small; elevator jammed; gross lift computed badly; bulk of dirigible too much for her engine capacity; we almost scraped the roofs of Achy. This exorbitant scheme of carbon and hydrogen is absolutely wrong."

The official investigation of the disaster proved the truth of those facts and many others stated by the "Lieutenant Irwin." Achy, a tiny village, had not appeared in any report of the crash. *The hamlet was, however, on the very large map Flight Lieutenant Irwin was using.* A villager of Achy stated that the airship almost touched the church tower.

The experiments with carbon and hydrogen as a fuel were a military secret.

There seems little room for argument about the facts of the case. As to their interpretation, men will differ as their beliefs and philosophies differ.

One mind once knew all the facts stated by Mrs. Garrett—that mind went beyond the final question mark in a moment of flame and fog, of buckled girders and ripping fabric, when the R-101 ended her shadowed destiny.

Whatever the solution of the enigma, it is certain that death is one mystery that can baffle no man forever.

Index

INDEX

INDEX

INDEX

INDEX

INDEX